Marcus,

Thank you for the super support!

Best wishes →

Kim Henne

Valuation of Human Capital

Kimberly K. Merriman

Valuation of Human Capital

Quantifying the Importance of an Assembled Workforce

Kimberly K. Merriman
Manning School of Business
University of Massachusetts Lowell
Lowell, MA, USA

ISBN 978-3-319-58933-6   ISBN 978-3-319-58934-3   (eBook)
DOI 10.1007/978-3-319-58934-3

Library of Congress Control Number: 2017944545

Cover Illustration: © Stephen Bonk/Fotolia.co.uk

Printed on acid-free paper

This Palgrave Macmillan imprint is published by Springer Nature
The registered company is Springer International Publishing AG
The registered company address is: Gewerbestrasse 11, 6330 Cham, Switzerland

Dedicated to the scholars, business professionals, colleagues and other smart people whose contributions to the field helped shape this book.

Contents

ABOUT THE AUTHOR

Kimberly K. Merriman is a Management Professor with the Manning School of Business at UMass Lowell, an innovative educator, business advisor and a widely published and cited authority on compensation, performance management, and human capital. She holds a Ph.D. in Organizational Management and Human Resources and a B.B.A. in Accounting. She can be reached at http://www.kkmerriman.com.

LIST OF FIGURES

LIST OF TABLES

Preface

Abstract This chapter provides an overview of the author's background, qualifications and perspective on human capital. It outlines the book's purpose, what readers can expect to gain and a description of each chapter's content. In short, human capital is defined for this book's purpose as the organization's assembled, trained and experienced workforce. In keeping with the author's experience, the material is grounded in scholarly research and practitioner based knowledge, providing readers with a conceptual and applied understanding of approaches to human capital valuation. This chapter also clarifies what the book is not—that it is not an accounting approach, per se, to the valuation of human capital.

Keyword About the author · Book overview · Human capital valuation

This book is a foundational guide to the valuation of an organization's human capital. Many would agree it is the people that make the organization. This is especially true in a knowledge economy, where an assembled, trained, and experienced workforce is typically considered a company's greatest asset. Yet few organizations actually evaluate their workforce in these economic terms. To address this void, presented herein is a way to understand the economic value of human capital for the firm and, in the process, a financial view of the assembled workforce

© The Author(s) 2017
K.K. Merriman, *Valuation of Human Capital*,
DOI 10.1007/978-3-319-58934-3_1

beyond the traditional accounting treatment of workers as an operating expense.

The book begins by highlighting the paradigm shift involved in viewing workers as a human capital asset versus simply a cost. The remaining chapters present ways to conceptualize and quantify the value of human capital for organizational decision-making and discretionary reporting purposes. The material is grounded in scholarly research and practitioner-based knowledge. Clear language is applied to a complex subject so students, professionals, and scholars of all levels of familiarity with the topic will benefit. Readers will finish with an understanding of approaches for the valuation of a firm's human capital, practical applications for the economic analysis of human capital, and gaps that are ripe for research and practice to address.

The author, Kimberly K. Merriman, is a Management Professor with the Manning School of Business at University of Massachusetts Lowell, an innovative educator, scholar, business advisor, board member, and widely published and cited authority on compensation and performance management. She holds a Ph.D. in Organizational Management and Human Resources and a B.B.A. in Accounting. She is also credentialed as a Certified General Appraiser.

Prior to entering academia, Kimberly worked for a dozen years as a valuation consultant in commercial real estate. The valuation of the assembled workforce has played an interesting role in commercial real estate appraising. Commercial properties are typically valued based on highest and best use as a going business concern—a "real property going concern" value. Thus the estimated value of a hotel building or nursing home facility, for example, relies on the value of the operating business. The real estate is integral to the business and, in many cases, income generated from the real estate and the business that occupies it are intertwined and essentially inseparable. There are occasions though, such as with real estate tax assessments, that the value of the real estate must be isolated from the value of the non-realty business assets. It is in these instances that appraisers have sought to identify and deduct the value of the assembled workforce from the overall real property going concern value. The author provides practical insights from her experience in this area throughout several chapters, especially when discussing the cost approach to human capital.

1.1   A Closer Look at What This Book Offers

From a theoretical perspective, ascribing economic value to a firm's human capital was an idea inherent in the basic but profound question put forth by scholars over 45 years ago:

> Suppose that tomorrow your firm had all of its present facilities—everything, but no personnel except the president; and he had to rebuild the human organization back to its present effectiveness. How much would this cost?[1]

Scholars and practitioners alike still wrestle with this question today. Little substantive progress has occurred to address the valuation of human capital in a consistent, practical, and accessible way. Yet it is a particularly timely question given the growing disconnect between the market value and "book" value of businesses.

In parallel, the science of workforce analytics has emerged to bring a more precise, quantitative, and empirically driven lens to a wide range of human capital issues. The data and analytical capacity to examine and influence human capital value arguably exist more so today than ever in the past. Yet the *theoretical justification, conceptual logic, and practical understanding of how to do so* are not sufficiently fleshed out.

To address these points, this book offers conceptual perspectives on human capital valuation *and* provides readers with a practical understanding of current approaches to the valuation of an assembled workforce. In detailing accepted methods for valuation, it provides well-defined steps for three distinct approaches: cost approach, market approach, and income approach. Discussion of each method includes its advantages and disadvantages, clear examples, and theoretical underpinnings.

It is also important to distinguish what this book is not. This is not an accounting approach, per se, to the valuation of human capital. Accounting standards vary by country and shift over time. In addition, values that are derived for accounting purposes may require artificial numbers that are not in keeping with actual "market" value. In some cases, accounting terms and treatment are referred to throughout chapters when it is relevant to do so, and at times the accounting treatment is not inconsistent with the market value of human capital.

In sum, there is a glaring gap between the espoused importance surrounding organizational human capital (the assembled, trained, and experienced workforce) and the actual assessment and reporting of human capital value. The overarching goal of this book is to provide the fundamental knowledge and techniques that will help reduce this gap. The book is designed to be an accessible, methods-based manual for the valuation of human capital and one that is relevant for teaching, applied research, and practice. It is distinct from other books currently available in that it integrates a widely diffused amount of information on the valuation of human capital into one succinct source.

1.2   OVERVIEW OF CHAPTERS

Chapter 2 describes the shifting perspective of human capital over time and how it is now increasingly considered an important business asset to be quantified. It discusses the current and potential uses of human capital measurement, introduces and defines basic terms that are essential to understanding human capital valuation, and generally sets the stage for the subsequent chapters.

Chapter 3 provides an overview of the basic logic and steps involved in applying the cost approach. The cost approach is based on the economic principle of substitution, which equates the value of human capital to the cost to create a substitute workforce of comparable utility. Costs considered in applying this valuation method to the assembled workforce pertain to recruitment, hiring, training, lost productivity, and entrepreneurial return. An illustrative example is provided. Further considerations and refinements of the cost approach are elaborated in Chap. 4. In addition to presenting the fundamentals of conducting the cost approach, this chapter discusses the conceptual reasoning and legal precedents that justify the cost approach as an acceptable, and actually preferred method for workforce valuations.

Chapter 4 provides further discussion of several key assumptions underlying the cost approach and suggests ways to add rigor to the cost evaluation. Many of these points were brought up throughout the preceding chapters in a cursory fashion. We delve into further detail here in order to gain a more critical understanding of the primary approach to valuing the assembled workforce. Specific topics include the conceptual rationale of the assembled workforce as an "owned" asset, a closer look at entrepreneurial return and lost productivity, refinements to workforce assemblage costs, and the special circumstances surrounding non-fungible and short-term workers.

Chapter 5 examines the income approach, an approach based on the economic principle of anticipation of future benefits. Under the income approach, valuation of human capital requires analysis of the expected net income stream directly attributable to the workforce. This chapter reviews several techniques for deriving the present value of the anticipated economic benefits of human capital. Economic benefits are measured as the value of worker outputs contributed to the firm, or alternatively via employee earnings as a proxy of the value employees contribute to the organization, and as the excess earnings remaining after allocating an appropriate amount of earnings to all other assets of the business. Also discussed is the conceptual logic of the income approach and its contrast with the cost approach, to highlight conceptual differences. While the cost approach is generally the preferred method for valuing the assembled workforce, the income approach is also practical when it is possible to quantify the income employees produce for the firm.

Chapter 6 examines the market approach to value, also known as the sales comparison approach. The market approach determines the value of an asset based on the selling price of comparable assets, in keeping with the economic principle of substitution. This chapter discusses the conceptual logic of the market approach applied to the valuation of human capital and reviews three potentially acceptable ways to value the assembled workforce through the market approach. The primary method reviewed is the residual market value technique, which allocates the acquisition price of a business to its different components. The two additional techniques considered are a value extraction method that compares sales that are similar in substantive ways with the exception of the assembled workforce in place, and the direct sale of an assembled workforce by itself.

Chapter 7 examines a basic but essential premise underlying the value of the assembled workforce. That is, for the workforce to have an ongoing value, its value producing properties must be sustained. The ongoing value of the assembled workforce is dependent on how the human resources are developed, trained, and employed going forward to maintain, enhance, or deplete the aggregate human capital value. The replacement cost of human capital considers the value at one point in time, after a workforce is assembled and at a stabilized level of performance.

To maintain this value requires proactive actions to prevent depreciation and obsolescence. This chapter draws from a range of research literature to describe four areas in which employer investment in employees is shown to impact employee performance contributions over the longterm: regeneration of physical and mental health, regeneration of viable skills, and maintenance of motivation.

Chapter 8 examines organizational social capital, an intangible asset embedded in the quality of the relationships among organizational members. Organizational social capital emphasizes the interconnections between the people that comprise the assembled workforce. It is thought to generate "relational wealth" for an organization by facilitating individual employee commitment to the collective good. This chapter defines and distinguishes the organization's social capital from its human capital, and discusses research on how social capital enhances the value of the assembled workforce. Also considered are ways organizations can develop social capital and the potential detractions to social capital value.

Chapter 9 provides an overview of other quantitative tools for understanding an organization's human capital. The previous chapters examined the overall value of the assembled workforce in place, which is the primary focus of this book. However, economic logic and quantitative measurement are also relevant to examining incremental changes in value associated with human capital practices and for informing human capital strategy decisions. In this chapter, we consider utility analysis, human capital metrics, and workforce analytics as ways to evaluate specific aspects of the workforce and human resource practices that ultimately have a bearing on the value of the firm's human capital.

NOTE

1. Likert, R. & Pyle, W. C. (1971). Human Resource Accounting: A Human Organizational Measurement Approach, Part II. *Financial Analysts Journal, 27*(1), 75–84.

Workers as an Asset vs. Cost

Abstract This chapter describes the shifting perspective of human capital over time and how it is now increasingly considered an important business asset to be quantified. It discusses the current and potential uses of human capital measurement, introduces and defines basic terms that are essential to understanding human capital valuation, and generally sets the stage for the subsequent chapters.

Keywords Human capital valuation · Human capital defined Intangible assets · Reporting human capital value

2.1 INTRODUCTION

What do an organization's workers represent? How someone answers this question is often a good indicator of their functional area of expertise. Accounting would typically answer in terms of operating costs. Finance is likely to reference productivity and efficiency metrics. Human resource professionals tend to emphasize turnover, tenure, and diversity when describing workers. Managers and leaders generally associate workers with performance objectives. To construe the assembled workforce—the firm's human capital—as a quantifiable business asset requires some integration from each of these areas along with input from the disciplines of economics and organizational behavior and strategy. You will gain a greater appreciation of this point as you read each chapter.

© The Author(s) 2017
K.K. Merriman, *Valuation of Human Capital*,
DOI 10.1007/978-3-319-58934-3_2

2.2   History of Perspectives on Human Capital

Human capital is broadly defined as the useful skills and knowledge individuals acquire to increase individual productivity and produce economic value.[1] There are a wide range of human capital definitions that further flesh out this basic definition. For example, when referring to a firm's assembled workforce in aggregate, the Society for Human Resource Management has suggested human capital is an asset representing "the collective sum of the attributes, life experience, knowledge, inventiveness, energy and enthusiasm that its people choose to invest in their work."[2]

One of the earliest references to human capital is found in Adam Smith's Wealth of Nations:

> Fourthly, of the acquired and useful abilities of all the inhabitants or members of the society. The acquisition of such talents, by the maintenance of the acquirer during his education, study, or apprenticeship, always costs a real expense, which is a capital fixed and realized, as it were, in his person. Those talents, as they make a part of his fortune, so do they likewise of that of the society to which he belongs. The improved dexterity of a workman may be considered in the same light as a machine or instrument of trade which facilitates and abridges labour, and which, though it costs a certain expense, repays that expense with a profit.

Nobel laureate Gary Becker is credited with bringing the study of human capital to the mainstream with what has come to be known as human capital theory.[3] He studied investments in human capital, such as schooling and on-the-job training and medical care "that influence future monetary and psychic income by increasing the resources in people." The view represented by human capital theory suggests learning and experience directly increase worker productivity.[4] Signaling theory extends this notion to construe learning and experience as signals to potential employers of other valued but unobservable qualities.[5] For instance, attainment of a degree signals the general ability to persist at a difficult and long-term goal and provides employers a visible means from which to infer variation among potential employees.

The above lenses, human capital theory and signaling theory, incorporate a view of human capital from the individual level and societal level. Individuals seek a return on their investment in their own human capital and invest accordingly. At the broader level, human capital is a source of economic growth, which justifies the formation of social policy pertaining to human capital and societal level investment in education. This book considers human capital between these two levels of analyses—specifically focusing on the aggregate human capital within a firm and the value of this assembled and trained workforce.

2.3   A CALL TO INCLUDE HUMAN CAPITAL ON THE BALANCE SHEET

In a knowledge economy, human capital is a company's greatest asset. Yet you will not find it reported as an asset on the balance sheet, other than embedded in goodwill if the business was acquired at an amount in excess of the value justified by its tangible assets. Even then, an enhancement to goodwill captures the value of human capital at only one historic point in time. It does not account for additional investments by the company in workforce hiring, training, and development. At the same time, the *expenses* associated with these additional investments—the direct expenses associated with workforce compensation, hiring, training, and development—are explicitly accounted for on the financial statements, along with future obligations for retirement benefits and paid time off.

Many people have pointed out the conceptual disconnect in accounting practices that recognize and report human capital expenses but fail to recognize and report the full value of human capital assets. The disconnect is also quantifiably apparent in the significant gap between the market value of businesses and their book value—the value supported by regulatory accounting disclosure. The May 2016 Global Intangible Financial Tracker Report published by Brand Finance, an annual analysis of large public companies throughout the world with over 57,000 companies included, showed tangible business assets comprised only 53% of business market value in 2015. Intangible business assets, of which human capital is arguably a significant portion, represented the remainder.[6]

Nonetheless, historically and currently, the reporting of human capital as a business asset is not an accepted practice under standardized financial reporting standards throughout the world, including Generally Accepted Accounting Principles (GAAP), the standards that guide financial reporting in the USA. Companies are permitted to provide non-standardized, supplemental financial measures and information disclosure in their external reporting as a way to provide additional insights into interested parties such as investors. However, the reporting of human capital value is not particularly common even in that form, though this is slowly evolving.

For instance, the Institute of Management Accountants, a global association for accounting and finance professionals, has called for voluntary external reporting and use of internal reporting. And some companies are reporting metrics and qualitative indicators of worker value, even if not human capital value per se, toward signaling sustainable business performance—i.e., their ability to remain viable as a going concern over the long term. Independent ratings of corporate sustainability and social performance, by companies such as MSCI that track firm performance for institutional investors, provide indirect information on human capital value by reporting on categories that pertain to the firm's human capital, such as employee relations and diversity. In parallel with a growing awareness of human capital value, the science of workforce analytics has emerged to bring a more precise, quantitative and empirically driven lens to a wide range of human capital issues—thanks to advances in technology that have made the necessary data and analytical capacity more widely accessible.

2.4   Defining the Term Value

When we refer to human capital value, the "value" label means different things to different people and under different circumstances. In general, as alluded to above, "book value" is the historic cost of a business asset based on the price paid, whereas "market value" is the current price at which the asset can sell, which sometimes differs from the value determined under the accounting definition of "fair value." For the remainder of this book, we will focus on market value as our basis of value unless otherwise stated. However, the definition of market value is better understood by contrasting it with the definition of fair value. Therefore, we will briefly explore each definition.

The International Valuation Standards Council (IVSC) is an independent council of representatives from across the globe, formed to establish globally accepted asset valuation standards. The IVSC defines market value as:

> The estimated amount for which an asset or liability should exchange on the valuation date between a willing buyer and a willing seller in an arm's length transaction, after proper marketing and where the parties had each acted knowledgeably, prudently and without compulsion.[7]

More information pertaining to related definitions is found on the IVSC website at https://www.ivsc.org/ by searching their online Standards and Glossary. There you will also see two definitions of fair value, both of which suggest something less than the full market exposure inherent in the definition of market value, though the second definition of fair value is closer to the open-market assumption underlying market value:

> The estimated price for the transfer of an asset or liability between iden-tified knowledgeable and willing parties that reflects the respective inter-ests of those parties. For use in financial reporting under *International Financial Reporting Standards*, fair value has a different meaning: In IFRS 13 "Fair Value is the price that would be received to sell an asset or paid to transfer a liability in an orderly transaction between market participants at the measurement date."

Finally, fair value is also an officially defined term used by the Financial Accounting Standards Board (FASB), which is the independent board that establishes financial accounting and reporting standards for compa-nies that follow US. Generally Accepted Accounting Principles (GAAP). When used in this context, fair value is defined by FASB standard as a market-based measurement of value similar to the International Financial Reporting Standards or similar to market value:

> This Statement [Statement of Financial Accounting Standards No. 157] clarifies that the exchange price [fair value] is the price in an orderly trans-action between market participants to sell the asset or transfer the liability in the market in which the reporting entity would transact for the asset or liability, that is, the principal or most advantageous market for the asset or liability. The transaction to sell the asset or transfer the liability is a hypo-thetical transaction at the measurement date, considered from the per-spective of a market participant that holds the asset or owes the liability. Therefore, the definition focuses on the price that would be received to sell the asset or paid to transfer the liability (an exit price), not the price that would be paid to acquire the asset or received to assume the liability (an entry price).[8]

You can read the FASB standard in full and the latest updates to the standard through the FASB website (http://www.fasb.org/home) by searching their online FASB Reference Library. In sum, Fair Value and Market Value are sometimes aligned in a practical sense despite the former having a narrower definition pertaining to a more limited market or specific party in some cases. This book focuses on market value—the price that might be obtainable in the wider market.

2.5   Defining the Concepts of Intangible and Tangible Assets

In an accounting framework, a tangible asset is generally any business asset that has a physical form such as machinery, buildings and land, and inventory. The opposite of a tangible asset is an intangible asset or those assets that are not physical in nature, which includes such things as patents, trademarks, copyrights, and goodwill.[9] For instance, Forbes 2016 ranking of the world's most valuable brands shows that well-established trademarks such as Google, Coca-Cola, and Disney are more valuable than the actual current revenue generated by the brand.[10] One way to estimate the economic value of aggregate intangible business assets is to deduct the value of the tangible assets, which are more easily identified and quantified, from total market value. The remaining value is attributable to intangible assets. This follows the basic premise that the true value of a business is determined upon its sale.

Human capital is a specific type of intangible asset in that it is "unrecognized" for financial reporting purposes, as noted earlier. That is, unlike intangibles such as trademarks and patents, it is not permitted by accounting standards to have formal ascribed value in the financial statements. Instead, the value of human capital quietly exists within the general category of goodwill and, in some cases, in optional supplemental reporting. This treatment of human capital stems from long-held practices carried over from the industrial era, in which tangible assets reigned supreme in the creation of goods and services, unlike the contemporary knowledge-based economy in which businesses increasingly rely on intangible assets. It also stems from a belief that the quantification of human capital value is too difficult and subjective.

However, the Institute of Management Accountants (IMA), in a 2014 report titled Unrecognized Intangible Assets: Identification, Management, and Reporting, calls for greater attention to reporting of unrecognized intangible business assets, and especially human capital, noting that these assets have grown to represent the major source of corporate value.[11] IMA also notes the importance of intangible assets to long-term business sustainability. "While these type of assets fail to meet the criteria for recognition under current reporting standards, the identification, assessment, management, control, retention, and nurturing of these assets is necessary for an organization to maintain its capacity to operation."[12] Yet another reason, they suggest, to close the information gap on reporting of intangible assets.

2.6   EXTERNAL AND INTERNAL USES FOR VALUATION OF HUMAN CAPITAL

There a many entities that are interested in a company's financial status and sustainability, including the company itself (owners, shareholders, managers, and governance board) and others with a vested interest such as creditors, investors, employees, and labor unions. Independent rating agencies also scour this type of information in order to provide a source of consolidated data to the parties already mentioned and others. Essentially any smart investor and strategic decision-maker are likely to desire this information.

As discussed earlier, valuation of the assembled workforce is generally not permitted in financial accounting and reporting other than as a supplement to the required reporting. However, its valuation has a role in tax accounting in that the assembled workforce can be identified for amortization purposes after the merger or acquisition of a business. In this circumstance, a business owner might allocate a portion of the total acquisition price of the business to the assembled workforce in order to use its specific tax treatment. Identification of the value of the assembled workforce is also sometimes needed as an interim step in isolating the value of other intangible assets that require different treatments for accounting or reporting purposes. Because financial reporting and tax accounting standards vary across the globe and shift overtime, this book will not attempt to enumerate the regulatory standards. Instead, reference is made to standards only when relevant to illuminate the conceptual logic of human capital valuation.

Even though reporting of human capital value is not a regulatory requirement, financial statement users in practice cannot truly make well-informed decisions without information pertaining to the organization's human capital. For instance, if a business were to suddenly lose their workforce, not only would the value instantly decrease, but also the business may cease to exist altogether. Similarly, the value of the assembled workforce itself can be the driving factor in the acquisition of a business, particularly when workers are highly specialized or when labor markets are extremely tight for the skill set involved. As the Institute of Management Accountants points out in its 2014 report, statutory reporting requirements often lag the needs of the market. Through discretionary reporting, however, firms can provide valuable information on human capital value to serve stakeholder needs.

In addition, assembled workforce value is relevant in situations that require isolating tangible asset value from total market value, as needed for real estate (ad valorem) tax purposes in which intangible assets are generally exempt, and for some lending and insurance purposes that rely only on tangible asset value. Human capital value may also be used to estimate damages in lawsuits pertaining to breach of employment contract or aggressive "poaching" of a competitor's talent.

Finally, as alluded to initially, human capital value is relevant for internal organizational reporting purposes. It provides quantitative information to aid managerial decision-making in areas such as succession planning to protect asset value and it serves as a potential indicator of return on investment for human resource management decisions. Internal reporting may also make good use of qualitative information pertaining to human capital, and metrics pertaining to efficiency and quality. These additional human capital indicators are discussed in Chap. 9.

2.7   BRIEF OVERVIEW OF APPROACHES TO VALUE

In general, the same three established and accepted valuation approaches that are used to value businesses, real estate, and most types of assets—the cost, income, and market approach to value—are also used to value a firm's aggregate human capital. Translating these valuation techniques to the domain of human capital presents some unique challenges that will be discussed throughout. Chapters 3 through 6 detail the application of these three fundamental approaches to the valuation of the assembled workforce.

The cost approach is covered in Chaps 3 and 4. It is considered the primary method for valuing an assembled workforce and was accordingly given the most attention. The income and market approaches are covered in Chaps. 5 and 6, respectively. The remaining three chapters of the book focus on ancillary valuation considerations (sustaining human capital, Chap. 7, and the role of social capital, Chap. 8) and other quantitative views of human capital (Chap. 9).

The cost and market approaches are based on the economic principle of substitution, which equates the value of human capital to the cost to create or acquire a substitute workforce of comparable utility. The income approach is based on the economic principle of anticipation of future benefits, which suggests that under certain circumstances, valuation of human capital is possible through analysis of the expected net income stream attributable to the assembled workforce.

So even though human capital value is generally viewed as difficult to quantify, keep in mind that imperfect measurement has not kept other assets from regulatory and voluntary reporting. For instance, the current inventory of a business requires estimates of price, tangible assets such as buildings and equipment are subject to depreciation estimates, and accounts receivable require judgments on credit risk. The view underlying this book is that even an imperfect measure of human capital is highly useful as long as the value is based on reasonable assumptions that are explicitly identified.

2.8 CRITICAL THINKING QUESTIONS

1. Companies, managers, and leaders often state that people are their most valuable asset. A Dilbert cartoon made light of this cliché by having the manager realize he has been wrong all these years and instead employees are ninth on their list of valuable business assets. It turns out carbon paper ranks as eighth on the list. As funny as this is in a comic, it is only funny because it is so relatable. Do you think employees would feel more valued if companies actually measured and reported the value of the assembled workforce? Could doing so lead managers to treat employees differently, perhaps better? Is there a downside to explicit measurement and reporting of value for the assembled workforce—would some employees prefer not to be quantified as an asset?

2. This chapter discussed the disconnect in accounting practices that treat human capital as an expense and not an asset. Investments in tangible assets, on the other hand, are generally treated as an asset that is gradually depreciated over time rather than expensed all at once. Discuss the implications of this accounting difference for firm's that prefer to show higher short-term profits. Is a firm

in this case more likely to cut discretionary spending on human capital, which is recorded as an expense, or tangible assets that are recorded as an asset? What could this mean for the firm's long-term sustainability?

3. As an investor, discuss how you might use information on the value of a firm's human capital to influence your investment decision. In assessing human capital as an important factor of production, it has a distinction from tangible inputs that are directly controlled or owned by the organization. Ownership and control reduces the risk associated with the organization's ability to capture the future benefits generated by an asset. Human capital, on the other hand, resides in the individual workers and organizations do not have the same assurance over its future benefits as they might with owned assets—i.e., workers can generally leave the organization at will. What information about the workforce beyond the value of the assembled workforce might therefore be useful in assessing your investment risk?

Notes

1. Schultz, T. W. (1961). Investment in human capital. *The American Economic Review, 51*(1), 1–17.
2. Weatherly, L. A. (2003, September). The value of people: The challenges and opportunities of human capital measurement and reporting. *Society for Human Resource Management Research Quarterly.*
3. Becker, G. S. (1962). Investment in human capital: A theoretical analysis. *The Journal of Political Economy, 70*(5), 9–49.
4. Becker, G. S. (1993). *Human capital: A theoretical and empirical analysis, with special reference to education* (3rd ed.). Chicago, IL: University of Chicago Press for the National Bureau of Economic Research (Original work published 1964).
5. Spence, M. (1973). Job market signaling. *The Quarterly Journal of Economics, 87*(3), 355–374.
6. Brand Finance. (2016, May). *Global Intangible Financial Tracker.* http://brandfinance.com/images/upload/gift_report_2016_for_print.pdf. Accessed on 2 Feb 2017.
7. The International Valuation Standards Council. *Glossary.* https://www.ivsc.org/standards/glossary#letter_m. Accessed 1 Feb 2017.
8. Financial Accounting Standards Board. (2010). *Statement of Financial Accounting Standards No. 157.* http://www.fasb.org/jsp/FASB/

Document_C/DocumentPage?cid=1218220130001&acceptedDisclaimer= true. Accessed 1 Feb 2017.

9. Investopedia. *Tangible Asset*. http://www.investopedia.com/terms/t/ tangibleasset.asp#ixzz4EsKTYpzC. Accessed 1 Feb 2017.

10. Forbes. (2016). *The world's most valuable brands*. http://www.forbes.com/ powerful-brands/list/#tab:rank_header:revenue. Accessed on Feb 1 2017.

11. IMA. (2014). Statement of management accounting: Unrecognized intangible assets identification, management and reporting. Montvale, NJ: Institute of Management Accountants.

12. Ibid.

CHAPTER 3

Cost Approach to Value

Abstract This chapter provides an overview of the basic logic and steps involved in applying the cost approach. The cost approach is based on the economic principle of substitution, which equates the value of human capital to the cost to create a substitute workforce of comparable utility. Costs considered in applying this valuation method to the assembled workforce pertain to recruitment, hiring, training, lost productivity and entrepreneurial return. An illustrative example is provided. Further considerations and refinements of the cost approach are elaborated in chap. 4. In addition to presenting the fundamentals of conducting the cost approach, this chapter discusses the conceptual reasoning and legal precedents that justify the cost approach as an acceptable, and actually preferred method for workforce valuations.

Keywords Cost approach to human capital value · Human resource accounting · Replacement cost new of assembled workforce

3.1 INTRODUCTION

The cost approach is based on the economic principle of substitution, which equates the value of human capital to the cost to create or acquire a substitute workforce of comparable utility. Specific steps in the cost approach include identifying the costs involved in recruitment, selection and training of the workforce, and the additional costs associated with

© The Author(s) 2017
K.K. Merriman, *Valuation of Human Capital*,
DOI 10.1007/978-3-319-58934-3_3

an entrepreneurial return. As a precursor to these steps, the workforce is segmented and total compensation is estimated. Finally, the cost of an ideal replacement workforce (replacement cost new) is contrasted with the potentially suboptimal workforce in place to determine adjustments needed to reflect any existing depreciation or obsolescence in the current workforce assemblage. This chapter explains each of these steps for practical application.

3.2   ORIGINS OF THE COST APPROACH TO HUMAN CAPITAL VALUE

The essence of the cost approach to valuing the assembled workforce was formally put forth by research scholars Rennis Likert and William Pyle in 1971.[1] They posed a basic but profound question:

> "Suppose that tomorrow your firm had all of its present facilities— everything, but no personnel except the president; and he had to rebuild the human organization back to its present effectiveness. How much would this cost?"

These individuals along with others spearheaded by research centers within the University of Michigan were seeking to establish an interdisciplinary area of study and practice labeled human resource accounting. Their collective efforts integrated concepts from social science, finance, and accounting toward quantifying aspects of the organization's human resources. A 1969 published brief on the topic by R. Lee Brummet, Eric Flamholtz and Pyle discussed the logic behind capturing human resource value through its replacement cost.[2] They presented the actual investment to acquire and develop managerial employees as reported by a manufacturing firm under study.

Most relevant to the contemporary use of quantifying human capital value, as emphasized in this chapter, Brummet and colleagues discussed the utility of a replacement cost approach to estimate the "worth of the human capital assets" during the acquisition or merger of organizations. Replacement value in their description is determined by the estimated cost to recruit, hire, and train the acquired company's existing workforce, the cost to bring them to their present level of skill and familiarity with organizational operations, and the opportunity cost associated with foregone income during the time it would take to assemble and fully develop the workforce.

The historical acquisition cost associated with recruiting, hiring, training, and developing the assembled workforce was an initial accepted cost approach to human capital.[3] However, the more common approach applied today is the estimation of the replacement cost of the assembled workforce in current dollars in order to reflect the market's current assessment of value, and in keeping with the early work of Flamholtz.[4] Thus current applications of the replacement cost to value build on and still include certain elements from early models and, as we will discuss, also consider an additional entrepreneurial return not included earlier.

3.3 DOES COST EQUAL VALUE?

The cost approach considers the costs involved in acquiring an assembled and trained workforce—recruitment, selection and training costs, and any foregone income related to productivity loss during the training period. In one sense, it is considered a conservative approach to valuing a firm's human capital because it does not directly incorporate the potential additional value related to synergy among employees, and between employees and the organizational systems in which they are embedded. In another sense, the approach can inadvertently overstate value if cost estimates are derived from a firm that is inefficient in their approach to assembling a workforce.[5]

In a similar way of thinking, the cost to assemble and train a workforce is sometimes considered simply an investment in human capital rather than a reflection of the economic value of the firm's human capital. Economic value, it is suggested, should consider the anticipated future value of employee outputs for the firm.[6] However, this "expected value" approach to human capital valuation does not align with standard accounting practices that instead separate the acquisition value of an asset from the ongoing revenue it helps generate for the business. We will revisit this concept in the next two chapters.

Some court cases, described next, have argued that the value of the assembled workforce is already inherent in the financial performance of the company and reflected in the compensation expense. However, this overlooks the cost to assemble human capital. Such "sunk costs" are not evident in the ongoing financial performance of a company but would be evident as an added value in the sale price of a company, often encompassed within goodwill. In fact, the cost approach to human capital is now an accepted method for certain tax accounting purposes such as allocating a portion of the acquisition price of a company to the assembled workforce. The precedent-setting cases below provide further insight and support for the acceptance of this method.

3.4   LEGAL PRECEDENT

The value of the assembled and trained workforce is not recognized separately for U.S. financial reporting purposes. It is treated as an unidentifiable intangible asset for formal reporting purposes, although companies have increasingly engaged in supplemental reporting to convey information pertaining to the quality, quantity, and sustainability of their human capital. However, the value of the assembled and trained workforce is separately recognized for U.S. income tax accounting purposes and real estate tax assessment purposes in certain contexts—primarily as an allocation of value when a business transfers ownership in some fashion. Past legal decisions provide precedent for the recognition and handling of assembled workforce value in these circumstances. Below are three particularly relevant cases described in layman's terms, with a link to the full opinion for those interested in fuller and more technical detail.

3.4.1   *Ithaca Industries*

Ithaca Industries versus the Commission of Internal Revenue involved a filing with the United States Court of Appeals to reverse a decision in an income tax case.[7] The decision was granted on February 23, 1994 and set a precedent for recognition of the value of the assembled workforce as an intangible asset.

Ithaca Industries, Inc. (Ithaca) was a manufacturing company that transferred ownership in October 1983 through a merger to facilitate the retirement of the original company's founder. The business transferred for an amount of $110 million and was appraised at the time to determine how to allocate this overall value among certain acquired assets for income tax purposes—or in accounting terms, to determine the basis for depreciable and amortizable assets. The value ascribed to the assembled workforce, comprised 5153 line workers and 212 non-line employees, was $7.7 million.

When the U.S. Internal Revenue Service denied Ithaca Industries' income tax depreciation deduction, a court process ensued. The ultimate sticking point with the courts in this case, with regards to the assembled workforce, was whether it was appropriate and even possible to ascribe a shelf life to this asset. The initial trial outcome under the federal Tax Court was that an assembled workforce has no reasonably estimable limit in terms of useful years and was therefore not a depreciable asset, but rather simply part of the inseparable going concern value of the business (i.e., part of the ability of a business to generate income without interruption despite a change in ownership).

Ithaca Industries followed this decision with a court appeal in which they argued that not only could a reasonable value estimate for the assembled workforce be estimated, but a limited useful life could also be considered based on projections of employee attrition and skill depletion. A subtle point in all of this was that the assembled workforce at any given point in time required ongoing investments in recruiting and hiring—to address turnover—and training in order to maintain the utility of the assembled workforce as a collective. In other words, the ongoing regeneration of the assembled workforce requires substantial effort on the part of the business. The notion that the assembled workforce is not a self-regenerating asset laid the groundwork for its treatment as a depreciable asset.

The appeal court agreed in principle with the argument put forth by Ithaca Industries. Their view was that the value of the assembled workforce is maintained only through these continued investments. Therefore, the asset that results is new and distinct from the original workforce asset in place at the time of acquisition, because of the need for *effortful and costly* renewal to maintain a productive workforce. "Absent those efforts, the workforce as it was constituted on the date of the merger would have declined until there were no employees left in it." In fact, it is these types of expenses pertaining to recruiting, hiring, and training that formed the basis of value for the assembled workforce in the Ithaca Industries case and forms the foundation of the cost approach to human capital value in general.

The opinion resulting from the District Court appeal acknowledged clearly that a workforce has an ascertainable value and a limited useful life that meets the rationale of an amortizable asset. The further view of the Circuit Court Judge in reviewing this opinion was to agree with this concept, that the assembled workforce has a value and shelf life that can warrant amortization. However, whether the value and useful life were defensibly ascertainable was not a question of law, but rather up to the Tax Court to evaluate and try the facts regarding the sufficiency of the analytical methodology.

So in 1994, an important point emerged from the Ithaca Industries case, some 11 years after the original merger took place: The assembled workforce is a conceptually separable intangible business asset with a discrete useful life, though these are difficult to convincingly measure in practice.

3.4.2   *Burlington Railroad and Madonna Hotel*

The following two cases were in relation to reducing the real estate taxes of going concerns that have an inherent real estate component. The basic argument put forth by the business owner in each case was that the assembled workforce represents an intangible business asset that is distinct from the tangible asset value assessable for real estate tax purposes. The courts' support of this argument indicated recognition of a separable value for the assembled workforce and of the cost approach as a convincing means of determining this value.

Burlington Northern Railroad Company versus Bair, Director of Iowa Department of Revenue involved a filing with the United States Court of Appeals and was decided on July 6, 1995. The Department of Revenue had appealed the decision granted by the District Court that prohibited Iowa from collecting property taxes on the value attributable to intangible personal property, specifically stated to include the value of the assembled workforce. The Appeals Court upheld the favorable decision for Burlington Northern Railroad Company.[8]

A more recent case, ultimately settled in May 2014 through the U.S. Court of Appeals, occurred with the Ritz Carlton Half Moon Bay hotel in regards to real estate taxes assessed on the property value by the County of San Mateo, California. The operating hotel was acquired in 2004 for $124.35 million in total, and the assessed value was determined to be $116.98 million based on the county removing some intangible business assets from the real property value. Half Moon Bay argued that additional intangible business assets—including specifically the assembled workforce—be excluded from the real property value on which the assessment is based. This argument was supported by the court under appeal.[9]

3.5   REPRODUCTION VS. REPLACEMENT COST

The economic principle of substitution underlies the cost approach. This means a rational investor would pay no more for an asset than the cost to obtain or construct an equivalent asset. Cost in this case refers to all direct and indirect costs and adjustments for depreciation and obsolescence to derive a value for the existing asset. However, regardless of whether the asset in question is a tangible or intangible asset, the cost to reproduce an exact replica of the asset will typically differ from the cost to devise a functional equivalent.

Therefore, the first decision in applying the cost approach is between *reproduction* and *replacement* cost. Replacement cost is the most commonly applied approach to valuing the assembled workforce and the method we will focus on here. However, it is useful to understand the fundamental differences between the two means of determining the cost. As alluded to above, the reproduction cost is the cost of creating an exact duplicate of an existing workforce. The replacement cost is the cost of creating a workforce capable of matching the existing workforce in terms of productive output.

Since reproduction cost is an estimate of the cost to reproduce the exact same workforce currently in place, this amount could theoretically be determined by adding all costs to recruit, hire, and train the workforce in place and trending this amount to current-day dollars. I say theoretically because most companies do not track this information in sufficient detail to realistically do this. Further, it is difficult to estimate costs for learning and development that occurred organically or at the worker's own expense, which has enhanced the value of the workforce in place.

Reproduction cost focuses on the exact quantity and quality of the workforce in place. In doing so, it inherently overlooks obsolescence that may exist such as an excess number of workers. Replacement cost instead estimates the cost to replicate the functional utility of the workforce in place. It estimates this amount in current dollars and adjusts the costs as needed to reflect the potential superior utility of a replacement "ideal" workforce compared to the workforce actually in place. Thus in keeping with the economic principle of substitution, the replacement cost approach equates the value of human capital to the cost to create or acquire a substitute workforce of comparable utility, one that may look different from the current one in terms of number and quality of employees.

The following walks through the steps of the replacement cost method, including estimating developer's profit and entrepreneurial incentive, estimating physical depreciation and functional and economic obsolescence, and provides a practical example.

3.6   CALCULATING REPLACEMENT COST NEW (RCN)

The cost to recruit, train, and hire new employees of the same functional utility as the workforce in place can be estimated based on a percentage of employee compensation. In fact, replacement costs are commonly calculated as a function of employee compensation costs. This is a quicker approach compared to itemizing specific line item costs for recruiting, hiring and training, though not necessarily as accurate. However, as discussed in the next chapter, the numbers can be compared to benchmarks for replacement cost ratios as a reasonableness check. The basic steps for calculating replacement costs as a function of employee compensation follow in order. Tables 3.1 and 3.2 present an example of how these steps may appear in practice.

3.6.1   Number of Employees by Type

The first step is to determine the actual number of employees that comprise the assembled workforce and identify a meaningful categorization scheme for employee type. The categorization scheme should have relevance to the cost to recruit, hire, and train. For instance, determining the number of employees by functional area or job classification helps distinguish them with regards to level of training needed and difficulty of recruitment since costs can differ based on either of these factors. Other potential ways to segment employees include tenure on the job, education level, geography, recruiting channel (online or executive search firm), and more.[10]

3.6.2   Average Market Compensation

An estimate of average total compensation for each category of employee is needed in order to estimate replacement costs as a function of compensation. Total compensation includes base pay, variable pay such as bonuses and overtime, and employer-provided benefits. The actual compensation of the assembled workforce is a reasonable starting point. However, actual

Table 3.1 Example replacement cost new—Step 1

Employee level of responsibility	Number of employees	Average annual compensation[1] ($)	Average cost to recruit/hire[2] ($)	Average cost to train[3] ($)	Replacement costs new[4] ($)
Non-professionals	500	44,286	4,429	6,643	5,535,714
Entry-level professionals	150	64,286	9,643	6,429	2,410,714
Junior professionals	200	71,429	10,714	7,143	3,571,429
Senior professionals	150	92,857	13,929	4,643	2,785,714
Middle management	100	97,143	14,571	4,857	1,942,857
Executive management	10	171,429	42,857	8,571	514,286
Subtotal Replacement Cost New (RCN) assembled workforce					16,760,714

[1]Total compensation includes base pay, variable pay such as bonuses and overtime, and benefits estimated at 30% of total compensation
[2]Recruitment/hiring estimated as percentage of total compensation: non-professionals = 10%, professionals/management = 15%, executives = 25%
[3]Training estimated as a percentage of total compensation: junior professionals and below = 10%, senior professionals and above = 5%
[4]Replacement costs new = estimated cost to recruit/hire and train multiplied by number of employees

Table 3.2 Example replacement cost new—Step 2

Subtotal Replacement Cost New (RCN) assembled workforce		$16,760,714
Opportunity cost to developer		1,676,071
Opportunity cost of capital		586,625
Total Replacement Cost New (RCN) assembled workforce		$19,023,411
Less depreciation and obsolescence		
Physical depreciation	(e.g., amount actual compensation exceeds market compensation)	(951,171)
Functional obsolescence	(e.g., compensation costs of excess number of actual workers)	(139,286)
Economic obsolescence	(e.g., underfunded pension obligation)	(380,468)
Replacement Cost New Less Depreciation (RCNLD)		$17,552,486

rates of existing employees may vary from the current market rate required to replace the workforce with employees of comparable utility. A market survey of current rates is therefore needed to establish the appropriate rate. Various free sources of market compensation data exist including government agencies such as the U.S. Bureau of Labor and Statistics and online job sites such as Indeed and Salary.com.[11] These sources also provide information on the employer-provided benefits in order to calculate total compensation. A 2016 report by the Bureau of Labor Statistics indicates that benefits on average comprise just over 30% of the total compensation cost.[12]

3.6.3   Recruiting and Hiring Costs

An estimate of recruiting and hiring costs should include direct and indirect costs. Direct costs include advertising fees; fees to consultants for external support in recruiting; costs associated with screening, testing, and hosting candidates; relocation costs; hiring bonuses; and more. These costs will correlate to some degree with employee skill and ability level since higher level employees tend to require more extensive recruiting and screening efforts. Indirect costs include compensation (salary and benefits) for employees involved in recruiting and interviews, based on the amount of time devoted to recruiting versus other duties, and overhead such as office space and utilities. In analyzing this cost as a percentage of employee compensation, one study analyzing case studies of turnover over a 15-year period through 2007 found that recruiting and hiring costs for jobs paying $30,000 or less per year averaged just over 16% of compensation while jobs up to $75,000 per year were in the average range of 20%; highly specialized jobs and executive level positions could range much higher.[13] This report and other sources also provide costs per employee, which offers a means of checking the reasonableness of a percentage of compensation estimate. Care must be taken when referencing any benchmarks for recruiting and hiring costs to understand what is and is not included. For instance, the cited percentages above include initial training costs in some cases and are based on salary rather than total compensation. Job vacancy costs, particularly lost productivity, are also absent from the above and most benchmark estimates.

3.6.4   Training Costs

Similar to recruiting and hiring costs, training costs may include compensation for those employees involved in administering training, overhead costs in the form of office space and utilities for these employees, course materials, software or licensing fees for online training modules, course fees for training provided external of the organization, and other related costs. The lost productivity associated with new hires as they acclimate and develop proficiency, and in the form of salary and benefits paid to employees during training can comprise a large portion of this cost. However, lost productivity is often difficult to fully quantify. As a benchmarking source, Training Magazine provides an annual industry report analyzing training costs across a wide range of industries and positions.[14] Their reports indicate that companies generally spend more of their training budget on employees with lower levels of experience or skills.

3.6.5   *Entrepreneurial Return*

There are some differing views on terminology and approach, but the common logic is that an assemblage creates an expected enhancement such that the final assembled workforce is worth more than simply its associated costs. Otherwise, a rational business owner would have little reason to pursue the assemblage when they could instead invest their expertise and capital elsewhere for a return. In economic terms, we must account for the opportunity costs associated with the factors of production—the resources or inputs used to produce the output. Classical economics recognizes three basic factors of production: land, labor, and capital. The latter two, labor and capital, are relevant factors of production in creating an assembled workforce. We can label these as the opportunity cost to the developer and the opportunity cost to the capital, for the analysis of calculating replacement costs for the assembled workforce. A more thorough discussion of how these two factors translate as a cost in determining the replacement cost new (RCN) of a workforce is provided in the next chapter.

3.7   REPLACEMENT COST NEW LESS DEPRECIATION (RCNLD)

So far we have calculated costs to create the workforce anew. However, our value estimate must reflect the current workforce in place, which may represent different forms of inefficiencies and depreciation compared to a new replacement workforce. The same depreciation concepts and terms that are established in association with tangible assets are applied to the assembled workforce. The concepts are translated below for the intangible domain of human capital.

It is important to clarify that any depreciation or obsolescence inherent in the actual assembled workforce that is curable—that can be eliminated from the workforce without cost—is *not* to be included in the depreciation deduction from replacement cost new. For instance, if actual pay rates are easily adjusted to market rates then the issue of overpaid employees is curable. In reality, however, it is very difficult to lower existing employee pay without incurring a cost to employee motivation and turnover to an extent that may exceed the value added. When viewed in this light, many if not most forms of identified depreciation and obsolescence would be classified as incurable and require a commensurate deduction from RCN in order to reflect the relatively less-valuable actual assembled workforce. This is the assumption made for the examples below.

3.7.1   *Physical Deterioration*

Physical deterioration pertains to the reduction in asset value due to continued use over time. In the case of human capital, this can manifest as disabled workers or workers that are near retirement and have a relatively short useful life remaining with the organization. It can also lead to workers that are over-qualified in terms of experience and potentially overpaid if pay increases outpaced the market rate for the job at hand—i.e., the job is done equally well by employees with less experience and lower pay. In all three cases, the RCN of the assembled workforce must be adjusted to reflect any incurable costs associated with these categories of workers that have an expected lower utilization rate or are overpaid relative to market rates. In other words, if someone were to purchase the business today, the employees on long-term disability, at near-term retirement and above market in pay, all represent an encumbrance of sorts that diminishes the value of the assembled workforce in place relative to the ideal workforce represented by replacement cost new.

3.7.2   *Functional Obsolescence*

Functional obsolescence considers if the number or types of actual workers are suboptimal compared to the workforce that would be established today, e.g., a new workforce may be more efficient and require fewer workers to accomplish the same work, or may warrant team leaders in place of middle managers if the workplace has shifted to become less hierarchical. In both cases, after establishing RCN for all actual workers in place, the costs associated with excess talent would be excluded from total replacements costs to derive replacement cost new less depreciation (RCNLD).

3.7.3 External Obsolescence

External obsolescence in the case of an assembled workforce pertains to a specific form known as economic obsolescence—the inability of the operations to generate a market-based rate of return on investment. Whereas the examples of physical and functional deficiencies discussed above are sometimes remediable through replacing workers, economic obsolescence is generally outside of the business owner's or investor's control. For instance, this can occur when the business is subject to employment contracts that exceed market terms—e.g., unions with advantageous collective bargaining agreements, faculty with tenure, and underfunded pension obligations. In these cases, RCN is adjusted to reflect the inherent economic loss and any remaining value represents (RCNLD).

In some cases, economic obsolescence will exceed RCN and then RCNLD for the assembled workforce is considered to have no value. The assembled workforce, under this situation, does not contribute a sufficient return to the business to justify it as an intangible asset. The business itself may have market value derived from its other assets and worker inputs, but the assembled workforce does not provide a contributory enhancement to this value beyond what is reflected in the revenue generated by the human capital—a market investor or buyer would not pay more for the privilege of an assembled workforce in this instance.

Critical Thinking Questions
1. A depreciation deduction to RCN is warranted when actual employee compensation is above market rates, as discussed earlier in this chapter. Therefore, the value of the assembled workforce is diminished when encumbered by above-market-pay commitments. Following the same logic, if actual employee compensation is below market rates, does this enhance the value of the assembled workforce? Reflect on why this would or why this would not make

the assembled workforce more valuable to a potential buyer of the business. Consider the risk of employee turnover and potential effects for employee motivation in analyzing this question.

2. Discuss how you would cure the functional obsolescence of an assembled workforce in regards to an excess number of employees. Is this form of obsolescence easily cured? What are the potential direct and indirect costs involved in reducing the workforce to the ideal size? Do the costs exceed the value added? In other words, are there times when the issue of excess employees represents a form of incurable functional obsolescence?

3. Investments in training represent a significant part of the value of the assembled workforce since the total costs associated with employee training are significant. Does online training that is automated and self-directed have potential to minimize training costs and therefore reduce the role training plays in the value of an assembled workforce? Consider the direct and indirect costs, particularly lost productivity, when analyzing this question.

NOTES

1. Likert, R., & Pyle, W. C. (1971). Human Resource Accounting: A Human Organizational Measurement Approach, Part II. *Financial Analysts Journal, 27*(1), 75–84.

2. Brummet, R. L., Flamholtz, E. G., & Pyle, W. C. (1969). Human Resource Accounting: A tool to increase managerial effectiveness. *Management Accounting, 51*(2), 12–15.

3. Pyle, W. C. (1970). Human resource accounting: Part I. *Financial Analysts Journal, 26*(5), 69–78.

4. Flamholtz, E. (1973). Human resources accounting: Measuring positional replacement costs. *Human Resource Management, 12*(1), 8–16.

5. Cascio, W. F. (1999). *Costing human resources: The financial impact of behavior in organizations* (4th ed). Cincinnati, OH: South-Western Educational Publishing.

6. Flamholtz, E. (1999). *Human resource accounting: Advances in concepts, methods, and applications* (3rd ed). Norwell, MA: Kluwer Academic Publishers.

7. Ithaca Industries, Inc., Appellant, v. Commissioner of Internal Revenue, Appellee, 17 F.3d 684 (4th Cir. 1994). Retrieved from http://law.justia. com/cases/federal/appellate-courts/F3/17/684/566900/ and http:// www.allcourtdata.com/law/case/ithaca-industries-inc-v-commissioner-of-internal-revenue/cA5xdj8?page=1.

8. Burlington Northern Railroad Company, Inc., Appellee, v. Gerald D. Bair, Director of Iowa Department of Revenue, Appellant, 93–4029 (8th Cir. 1995). Retrieved from http://caselaw.findlaw.com/us-8th-circuit/1198525.html.
9. SHC Half Moon Bay, Plaintiff and Appellant, v. County of San Mateo, Defendant and Respondent, A137218 (Cal. App. 1st Dis. 2014). Retrieved from http://caselaw.findlaw.com/ca-court-of-appeal/1667663.html.
10. American National Standards Institute, Inc. (2012). *Cost-per-Hire Standard.* Alexandria, VA: Society for Human Resource Management. Retrieved from https://www.shrm.org/ResourcesAndTools/business-solutions/Documents/shrm_ansi_cph_standard.pdf
11. Online sources for data on market compensation include the U.S. Bureau of Labor Statistics https://www.bls.gov/bls/blswage.htm, Indeed https://www.indeed.com/salaries, and Salary.com http://salary.com/.
12. U.S. Bureau of Labor Statistics (2016, September). *Employer costs for employee compensation.* Retrieved from https://www.bls.gov/news.release/pdf/ecec.pdf.
13. Boushey, H., & Glyn, S. J. (2012, November). *There Are Significant Business Costs to Replacing Employees.* Center for American Progress. Retrieved from https://www.americanprogress.org/issues/economy/reports/2012/11/16/44464/there-are-significant-business-costs-to-replacing-employees/.
14. Training Magazine. (2015, November/December). *2015 Training industry report.* Retrieved from https://trainingmag.com/trgmag-article/2o15-training-industry-report.

CHAPTER 4

A Closer Look at Cost Approach Assumptions

Abstract This chapter provides further discussion of several key assumptions underlying the cost approach and suggests ways to add rigor to the cost evaluation. Many of these points were brought up throughout the preceding chapters in a cursory fashion. We delve into further detail here in order to gain a more critical understanding of the primary approach to valuing the assembled workforce. Specific topics include the conceptual rationale of the assembled workforce as an "owned" asset, a closer look at the entrepreneurial return and lost productivity, refinements to workforce assemblage costs, and the special circumstances surrounding non-fungible and short-term workers.

Keywords Lost productivity of assembled workforce
Entrepreneurial return on assembled workforce
Depreciation of human capital · Obsolescence of human capital

4.1 INTRODUCTION

There are five topics of particular interest that are covered for this purpose. First is a conceptual elaboration of how the assembled workforce represents an "owned" asset, when in reality people are not owned. Next is a more detailed explanation of the components of entrepreneurial return, followed by an accounting of lost productivity—both are a significant part of the cost to assemble a workforce and two of the more complex aspects of the cost analysis. This is followed by ways to refine the accuracy of costs in general, including hiring, recruiting, and depreciation costs. Finally, the fungibility of employees is considered. The replacement cost approach implicitly assumes employees are replaceable, i.e., fungible. Some exceptions are discussed by the example of certain employees that are not interchangeable.

4.2   People Are not Owned

When applied to people as assets, it is important to distinguish between the value inherent in assembling a workforce versus ownership of the actual human capital—i.e., ownership of the people who constitute the workforce. Whereas the firm does not "own" human capital, "the attributes of *an assembly of people* with special skills, team-working ability, pride of workmanship, or loyalty can be a valuable intangible business asset."[1] This point is supported by legal precedent, as described in the previous chapter.

The cost approach for a trained and assembled workforce seeks to capture the cost to replace or reproduce the workforce in place—recruitment, hiring, and training of the workforce. Note that it intentionally does not include the value of the human capital that resides within the individual. This value is owned by the employee, which is free to leave the position and take their human capital with them, and is only "rented" by the employer via the compensation paid to its workers. Employees lend their ability to a workplace that in exchange pays "rent" in the form of compensation to use this resource.

Also, the value of the human capital that is embedded in the employee is presumably already reflected in the firm's revenue since the worker's human capital contributes to this revenue. This notion is consistent with accounting concepts in that compensation expenses are deducted from revenues under financial and tax accounting standards. Its consistency with accounting principles makes the cost approach the common means in the valuation of an assembled workforce. The related components that comprise the overall value of an operating business are depicted in Fig. 4.1.

4.3   Understanding Entrepreneurial Return

The steps to calculating replacement costs in the prior chapter included an entrepreneurial return, based on the logic that an assemblage creates an expected value enhancement over and above its associated costs.

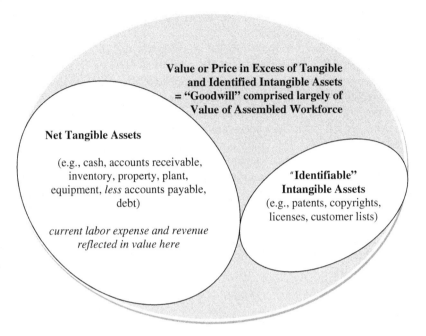

Fig. 4.1 Business value components

Otherwise, a rational business owner would have little reason to pursue the assemblage when they could instead invest their expertise and capital elsewhere for a return. This return was described in terms of the opportunity cost to the developer and the opportunity cost to the capital. While there are some differing views on terminology and approach, the following provides insight to the underlying rationale for calculating and including these additional costs.

4.3.1 Opportunity Cost to the Developer

Per the Appraisal Institute's recommendation on valuing intangible assets, "a developer can be thought of as a special class of labor, making the development fee a special class of wage," and is therefore entitled to receive their opportunity costs in exchange for their contribution to creating the asset.[2] This reasoning assumes the developer of the intangible asset has a profit motive. In valuing human capital, it essentially represents a return on the business owner's investment of time and effort in assembling the workforce.

This return is commonly labeled developer's fee or profit, though the term profit can confuse it with the additional level of *economic profit* associated with entrepreneurship that is realized after the sale as a residual value after all other costs, including the return to labor and capital, are satisfied. With economic profit, the entrepreneur receives what, if anything, is left over. This speculative return is typically not included in the cost approach.

The opportunity cost to the developer, or developer's fee, is typically calculated as a percentage rate of return of total direct and indirect costs, at a rate in keeping with industry norms. Therefore, in valuing a firm's human capital, the developer fee is calculated as a percentage rate of return on the total costs associated with the workforce assemblage, at a rate in line with the prevailing terms of the market for a development initiative of equivalent effort and risk.

4.3.2   Opportunity Cost of Capital

The opportunity cost of capital is sometimes referred to as entrepreneurial incentive—the return required to persuade an individual to pursue the investment. However, again, this should not be confused with the residual economic profit described above, which is the speculative amount that the assembled workforce may transfer for over and above its total costs. The logic underlying inclusion of this cost in valuing human capital is that a return on capital invested to build the workforce is only gradually realized as the workforce becomes assembled and trained. A buyer of a business with the workforce already in place and fully trained earns a return from day one, and would therefore pay a higher value for this privilege.[3]

Robert F. Reilly, a managing director with the business valuation firm Willamette Management Associates, provides one of the more cohesive explanations of this particular cost that I have come across: "The lost income concept of entrepreneurial incentive can be considered in the context of a make-versus-buy decision."[4] In other words, if a workforce is made rather than acquired as part of a going concern, there is lost income (lost return on capital invested) over the duration of time involved in assembling and training the workforce. This lost income can be calculated as an opportunity cost of capital by applying an appropriate rate of return to the *average* total direct and indirect replacement cost investment over the assemblage period. For instance, if the full assemblage and training of the workforce takes one year to complete, the average cost throughout that year can be estimated at half the total cost. Implicit in this is not all costs are incurred at once and returns are gradually experienced leading up to stabilization at year end. The rate of return applied should be based on the cost of capital, that is, the rate of return that could be earned by placing the money in a different investment of equivalent risk.

4.4   Lost Productivity

As noted in the previous chapter, often the costs associated with recruitment and training that are referenced in benchmarked sources or tracked internally within the organization do not include the cost of lost productivity, even though it can represent a significant amount. Lost productivity is an opportunity cost rather than an amount paid out, and therefore difficult to quantify and sometimes not perceived as a cost. It occurs in two forms, as the lost productivity while the position is vacant and while new hires undergo training or other forms of formal and informal on-the-job learning that is required to reach full productivity, categorized respectively as part of recruitment costs and training costs.

An accurate estimate of lost productivity related to training requires consideration of the varied learning curves across employees. The amount of time entailed in hiring, employee learning, and the pace of productivity improvements commonly varies across job categories and seniority of the position. Estimates can be derived from actual company experience and market data to allow for an average by employee segments. The rate would be expressed as a percentage of the total compensation with the implicit assumption that employees are paid their marginal product (i.e., pay equals what employees contribute in value to the organization).

For example, engineers may take on average a year to hire and reach full productivity. Productivity is at 0% while the position is vacant. The new hire may start at 60% productivity and then gradually increase to full productivity. While a discounted cash flow template could be made to analyze the present value of the precise loss to productivity as it incrementally changes over the total time period in question, the assumptions underlying this degree of precision would be difficult to defend. Instead an average rate of loss for the workforce segment is appropriate. For example, if employees take 3 months on average to hire and 9 months to reach full productivity after hire, lost productivity would equate to 40% of total compensation: A 100% productivity loss for 25% of the year plus a 20% average productivity loss for 75% of the year.

Note that these costs associated with foregone productivity are an additional opportunity cost incurred over and above the entrepreneur's opportunity cost of capital described in the previous chapter. These added costs enhance the value of the trained and assembled workforce since they represent costs that a new owner of the business would not have to incur. Said another way, due to the integral nature of the workforce to the revenue of the business, any deficiency in the assemblage or training of the workers translates to lost value.

4.5   REFINING AND SUPPORTING WORKFORCE ASSEMBLAGE COSTS

The previous chapter provided guidelines for estimating the costs associated with assembling a workforce. Following are several suggested ways to bolster the accuracy and defensibility of these calculations.

4.5.1   Recruitment, Hiring, and Training Costs

The previous chapter emphasized the use of external benchmarks and market averages in estimating recruitment, training, and hiring costs. It is also useful to compare the actual costs incurred by the organization in question as a point of comparison and as a potential bolster to the validity of market estimates. It is important, however, to capture all actual costs when doing the cost analysis. External benchmarks make this easier in some regards since the costs are already surveyed and hopefully contain the full range of costs entailed. Familiarity with some of the less obvious costs can help in evaluating both internal and external information for completeness.

The Society for Human Resource Management (SHRM) partnered with American National Standards Institute (ANSI) to develop a standardized format for calculating cost per hire.[5] They include external costs associated with recruiting and hiring that are charged by vendors and third-parties, such as advertising, consulting, and outsourcing fees, and internal organizational costs such as the compensation for employees involved in the recruiting and hiring process. The intention of this collaboration was to standardize what was otherwise a varied and subjective evaluation across organizations. Some of the less frequent and therefore potentially overlooked costs in recruiting and hiring cited by the SHRM/ANSI cost-per-hire standard include signing bonuses, employee referral awards, internal overhead for monitoring and reporting of government compliance, recruiting learning and development costs, and costs associated with the technology used to support the process.

With regards to training, the evaluation must go beyond the direct and indirect costs of formal modes of training such as class instruction, on-the-job training, and orientation to include workplace integration costs. This includes the cost to fit new employees into the right work team and equip the employee with the needed equipment and resources for the job such as computer, software, company email address, office phone number, office furnishings, and more.[6]

4.5.2   *Depreciation and Obsolescence*

Allowances for depreciation and obsolescence consider characteristics of the actual assembled workforce that are inferior or inefficient compared to the ideal workforce that would be hired today. As discussed in the prior chapter, these differences call for adjustments to derive the value of assembled workforce in comparison to the calculated replacement cost new. A primary cause for adjustment is when actual employees are paid more than market rates. That is, certain employees may be replaceable with a lower paid employee of equal utility. As described earlier, this represents a form of physical depreciation. If the job is done equally well by employees with less experience at a lower pay rate, the value of the assembled workforce must be adjusted to reflect its less than ideal state. In fact, it is quite common for employee pay rates to be out of step with market rates, particularly for longer tenured employees.

The comparison between internal pay rates and market rates becomes more difficult to reconcile when companies emphasize individual performance in their pay scheme through significant merit pay, bonuses, or other forms of variable pay. Logic dictates that pay differences have some relation to performance in order to motivate and reward contributions, but attempts to single out individual performance will always have some degree of inherent flaw. Many businesses have accumulated a hodgepodge of random, arbitrary, and haphazard pay differences even among employees doing similar work. The problem is that once performance goes beyond the number of widgets produced or volume of sales made, it is really difficult to parse meaningful and objective differences between employees. Pay differentials are often more an art than a science, despite elaborate performance appraisal and compensation systems that give a sense of precision. And pay differentials persist even when reasonable precision is lacking because companies believe this is what works for motivating employees.

Therefore, in attempting to identify gaps between actual pay rates versus market rates, it could be useful to consider relative worth of the jobs or competencies in question within the organization before attempting to segment and match the assembled workforce to the market. Job evaluation is a process to determine the value of the position to the company—an internal pricing mechanism of sorts. While the job evaluation process is too lengthy and complex to pursue for the cost analysis alone, a company that has recently completed the job evaluation process for compensation purposes would have valuable information for use in the cost analysis of the assembled workforce. Calculation of the firm's revenue per employee is a relatively quickly calculated rule of thumb for evaluating actual internal compensation against market benchmarks to assess reasonableness and identify broad gaps. Specifics on how to calculate this metric and benchmarking sources are provided in Chap. 9, which discusses other quantitative views of human capital.

Evaluation of the marginal product (the change in output resulting from employing a unit of input, assuming all else remains constant) is another litmus test of whether current pay rates may exceed justification and therefore warrant a depreciation adjustment to the value of the assembled workforce. Pay in accordance with neoclassical economic theory should equal an employee's marginal product, that is, what an employee contributes in revenue to the organization. Therefore, if compensation per employee exceeds revenue per employee, compensation costs require close examination and the replacement cost new of the assembled workforce likely warrants a physical depreciation adjustment to reflect the costlier actual workforce in place, or possibly an adjustment for functional obsolescence to reflect the suboptimal efficiency of the actual workforce in place.

4.6   NON-FUNGIBLE AND SHORT-TERM WORKERS

With regards to human capital, we generally assume employees are a fungible asset—that substitutes of equal utility are readily available in the labor market. This assumption is essential to the cost approach to value and the calculation of replacement cost new. However, in instances of exceptional talent, this assumption is not valid. Company founders and certain CEOs may fall into this category. Company owners that are uniquely tied to their firm's image, such as Martha Stewart, are in this category. Nonexecutive employees that are star performers also meet this definition. Star performers are those employees that contribute exceptional output consistently over time relative to the productivity of others, and whose departure would have a significant negative impact on organizational productivity.[7] Star employees are reasoned as more common in the twenty-first-century knowledge economy, enjoy greater job mobility due to their star qualities, and require considerably higher pay than the average employee in order to retain.[8] The presence of star employees must be carefully considered when valuing an assembled workforce since they add disproportionate value and disproportionate risk to the equation at the same time.

Finally, a very different type of employee should also receive careful consideration. Short-term workers that are hired contingent based on a narrowly defined length of time or set of objectives are not typically suited for inclusion in the value of the assembled workforce. The value inherent in the assembled workforce derives from the anticipated relative stability of the trained workforce and its ability to continue generating revenue for the business without interruption. Workers that are subject to frequent replacement do not provide this economic benefit and pose an ongoing cost to recruit, hire, and train new workers at a greater level than the turnover rate associated with more standard employment arrangements. The cost approach to value does not typically recognize value for this segment of an assembled workforce. However, these types of employment relationship are on the rise and are epitomized in the form of "gig" and "on-demand" workers. Valuation models will undoubtedly need to evolve over time to reflect the changing landscape surrounding work relationships.

4.6.1 Critical Thinking Questions

1. The cost approach to valuing the assembled workforce relies on the assumption that individual employees are replaceable without diminishing the value of the whole assemblage. As we discussed in this chapter, there are exceptions to this assumption in the upper echelon of the organization (e.g., certain CEOs) or in the field

of sports where certain top athletes are seen as irreplaceable. Can you think of other examples of critical employees throughout the organizational hierarchy whose replacement would significantly diminish assembled workforce value? For instance, consider businesses that rely on scientific innovation or businesses that rely on relationships built over time between the employee and client/customer. How might you evaluate the irreplaceability of employees in these circumstances?

2. A common and impactful human capital decision faced by all businesses is the make-versus-buy decision, that is, the decision of whether to hire someone with the needed knowledge, skills, and abilities at a commensurately higher compensation versus someone without these qualities for lower compensation and then train and develop them over time. Consider how the cost of lost productivity, as discussed in this chapter, can inform and influence this decision.

3. The opportunity cost of labor and capital entailed in developing an assembled workforce are sometimes difficult to solidly conceive. Relate these two costs to a different endeavor to gain and demonstrate greater clarity. For example, consider a sole inventor that devoted one year to creating a new and better mousetrap. What is this inventor's opportunity cost in terms of labor (time and effort that could have been spent elsewhere)? If a family member paid the development costs of the mouse trap during its creation, what is the opportunity cost in terms of capital (the return that could have been earned if the money were invested elsewhere)?

NOTES

1. Appraisal Institute. (2011). *Fundamentals of Separating Real Property, Personal Property and Intangible Business Assets*. Chicago, IL: Appraisal Institute.
2. Ibid.
3. Reilly, R. F. (2013). Consideration of Functional and Economic Obsolescence in the Assessment of Industrial or Commercial Property. *Journal of Property Tax Assessment & Administration, 10*(1), 45–58.
4. Ibid.
5. American National Standards Institute, Inc. (2012). *Cost-per-Hire Standard*. Alexandria, VA: Society for Human Resource Management. Retrieved from

https://www.shrm.org/ResourcesAndTools/business-solutions/Documents/shrm_ansi_cph_standard.pdf.
6. Mueller, A. (2011, July). The cost of hiring a new employee. *Investopedia*. Retrieved from http://www.investopedia.com/financial-edge/0711/the-cost-of-hiring-a-new-employee.aspx#ixzz4WgEHFFcP.
7. Aguinis, H., & O'Boyle, E. (2014). Star performers in twenty-first century organizations. *Personnel Psychology, 67*(2), 313–350.
8. Ibid.

CHAPTER 5

Income Approach to Value

Abstract This chapter examines the income approach, an approach based on the economic principle of anticipation of future benefits. Under the income approach, valuation of human capital requires analysis of the expected net income stream directly attributable to the workforce. This chapter reviews several techniques for deriving the present value of the anticipated economic benefits of human capital. Economic benefits are measured as the value of worker outputs contributed to the firm, or alternatively, via employee earnings as a proxy of the value employees contribute to the organization, and as the excess earnings remaining after allocating an appropriate amount of earnings to all other assets of the business. Also discussed are the conceptual logic of the income approach and its contrast with the cost approach.

Keywords Income approach to human capital value · Lev and Schwartz model · Flamholtz stochastic rewards valuation model · Capitalized excess earnings method

5.1 Conceptual Logic of the Income Approach

The income approach to value explicitly considers the future quantity and quality of an income stream, including its risk and likelihood of continuity. This is distinct from the cost approach, which does not entail future projections. The cost approach instead accounts for the present

K.K. Merriman, *Valuation of Human Capital,*
DOI 10.1007/978-3-319-58934-3_5

quality of the asset through adjustments for depreciation and obsolescence, and implicitly assumes an ongoing investment to maintain the present value of the assembled workforce. By considering risk and return of an income stream over a holding period, the income approach is more in keeping with the typical investors way of analyzing value. Ascribing future income streams to human capital, however, involves many subjective assumptions that can render the income approach in this domain more complex and less reliable than the cost approach.

The income approach for intangible assets such as human capital generally follows the same steps as when applied to tangible assets such as an office building. The distinction with the assembled workforce is the need to isolate the value of one part of a larger whole. The workforce is an asset that is integral to the income and value of the larger overall business, but the intertwined nature makes it difficult to quantify the portion of business income that is attributable strictly to the workforce.

Attempts to isolate the portion of business income attributable to the firm's human capital take several forms. The amount paid in compensation may serve as a proxy for the firm earnings that are attributable to the workforce. In some cases, such as with a salesforce, it may be possible to directly assess the amount of earnings the firm derives specifically from the workforce. A residual method first identifies the portion of firm earnings implied by the value of tangible assets and other identifiable intangible assets and attributes the remaining or "excess" earnings to the assembled workforce. Once an income attributable to the workforce is established, this income is converted into present value through capitalization or discounting. Various approaches that apply these concepts are discussed in order below.

5.2   CAPITALIZATION OF AGGREGATE COMPENSATION TECHNIQUE

One straightforward approach is to capitalize the aggregate compensation of the assembled workforce. Workers are presumably paid at or near the value they contribute to the organization and therefore compensation is a reasonable proxy for estimating the income attributable to human capital. Basic economic theory states that firms pay workers only up to the point where marginal labor costs equal the economic value associated with the marginal product of labor. In simple terms, firms pay employees no more than the value employees generate for the firm. This is known as the marginal revenue productivity theory of wages.[1] This sets the compensation ceiling, at least in theory, whereas the competitiveness of the labor market sets the compensation floor. In practice a firm may have reason to temporarily pay above the marginal product of labor, or may simply be unable to accurately identify the marginal product. As with all techniques, there are recognized limitations in using compensation as a proxy for human capital value.

A capitalization rate represents the return the investor expects to receive based on market parameters, and numerically is simply the ratio of income to asset value. Income for a single period—normally 1 year—is capitalized into an overall present value by dividing the income by the capitalization rate. For example, an 8% capitalization rate and an aggregate annual salary of 1 million dollars indicate a value for the assembled workforce of 12 million dollars.

An inherent assumption when capitalizing income is that the asset has an indefinite useful life and therefore the income stream continues in perpetuity. An assembled workforce meets this assumption if viewed as a replenishable group of workers whose value resides in the assemblage rather than within specific individual employees with varying useful lives. The logic and legal precedent for valuing the assemblage as a replenishable asset was discussed in Chaps. 3 and 4 with regards to the cost approach.

To reflect the assumption of perpetuity noted above, the income must be net of an allowance for the cost to maintain and replenish the asset. Net operating income is used as the basis for capitalization when valuing a tangible asset such as an office building. A net income equivalent for the assembled workforce would require deductions from total compensation for costs associated with employee turnover and ongoing training investments to maintain functional utility of the workforce. One could also argue for deductions related to management of the asset and more in order to mirror the template used in capitalizing value for tangible assets. Each deduction to income reduces the capitalized value further, of course.

5.3   THE LEV AND SCHWARTZ MODEL

The Lev and Schwartz model is based on the present value of employees' future earnings during their projected remaining years of service with the organization.[2] The model's original 1971 conceptual formulation estimated remaining service years based on a traditional retirement age of 65 and allowed for the probability of death occurring before retirement, to be drawn from independent actuarial tables. Employees were categorized into homogeneous groups based on skills and function, and then average earning profiles constructed for each group as a basis for projecting future earnings estimates. More specifically, estimates of future earnings for each remaining year of service were conceived as equivalent to current census data on earnings for the job classification and age in question to derive a *general* value of human capital, or estimated from profiling the actual pay structure within the firm, for firms with a large number of employees, to derive a *specific* value of human capital.

Earnings in this case represent a proxy for the value of the employees' estimated future contributions to the going business concern, following the principles of economic theory described earlier in the chapter. These future cash flows are discounted to present value at a rate equivalent to the cost of capital. Since the model focuses on the value of the remaining years of service for employees in place rather than the replenishable workforce assemblage with an indefinite useful life, there is no residual human capital value remaining beyond the projected discounted cash flow period. That is, the value of the workforce at the end of the projected service term is zero.

The Lev and Schwartz model has several limitations, some of which were acknowledged initially by the models originators and some through observations by others. The primary critique is the use of employee compensation as a proxy for employee contribution of value to the organization, which means the model focuses on employee inputs rather than employee outputs in the form of actual contributions to firm revenue. This is a potential shortcoming with any method that uses compensation as the measure for employee value contribution.

An additional issue specific to the Lev and Schwartz model is its focus on individual employees in place and their respective useful lives rather than treating the assembled workforce as a replenishable and indivisible asset. While each view of human capital can serve a distinct valuation purpose, the notion that the assemblage overall holds value for an indefinite term is in keeping with conceptual and legal precedent. Of course, an indefinite useful life also assumes ongoing investment to maintain the assembled workforce.

An advantage of the Lev and Schwartz model is its inherent consideration of the potential declining utility of a workforce in place due to shifts in desired skills, business processes, governmental regulations, or other factors. This is indeed likely to occur in the absence of ongoing investment to maintain human capital. Projecting an income stream over multiple periods for discounting to present value permits inclusion of periodic adjustments for ongoing declining utility, as in the present model, or adjustments for ongoing investments in human capital to maintain workforce utility. This level of fine-grained adjustment to the anticipated future income stream is not captured in direct capitalization approaches like the one presented earlier in the chapter.

5.4   THE FLAMHOLTZ STOCHASTIC REWARDS VALUATION MODEL

The Flamholtz stochastic rewards valuation model is similar to the Lev and Schwartz model in that it is also a discounted cash flow analysis that focuses on the individual employees in place rather than treating the assembled workforce as a replenishable and indivisible asset.[3] However, the Flamholtz technique attempts to measure anticipated economic benefits directly, as the value of employee outputs, rather than use compensation as a proxy. The value of each individual employee is based on the present value of projected outputs or services they will provide to the organization during their remaining useful life within the firm.

In estimating the future nature and value of employee outputs, consideration is given to how employee outputs may change over time as employees advance or change roles within the organization. In other words, employee trajectories are not assumed static, declining or necessarily linear at all. Probabilities are estimated for the potential trajectories to determine the likely value of future employee outputs. Organizational factors such as reward systems and opportunities for promotion or use of skills are assumed to influence employee trajectories and therefore influence the probability estimates for potential trajectories. Probabilities are also assigned to the likelihood of employees remaining within the organization throughout their productive career, essentially converting the useful life estimate to an estimate of the remaining term of the employment relationship.

The Flamholtz technique has a limitation in common with the Lev and Schwartz technique described earlier. By focusing on individual employees in place rather than treating the assembled workforce as a replenishable and indivisible asset, the human capital value derived represents only the actual employees and their discrete period of time with the organization, rather than recognizing the potential indefinite useful life of the assemblage. Strategic human capital research has more recently emphasized the organization's unique composition of human capital—essentially how its assembled workforce is structured—as an important source of human capital value that is complementary to, but beyond the human capital value that resides within individual employees.[4] Therefore, summing the value of individual human capital does not capture the full value of the workforce assemblage.

The Flamholtz technique also has an advantage in common with the Lev and Schwartz technique in using a discounted cash flow approach, which permits a level of fine-grained adjustment to the anticipated future income stream that is not captured in direct capitalization approaches. Further, the Flamholtz model overcomes the issue of using employee inputs, particularly compensation, as a proxy measure of the value generated for the organization by instead focusing firmly on employee outputs as the measure of economic benefit. However, projecting the expected revenue from employee outputs is often difficult and subjective. It is easier and more objective when the workforce is composed of employees in service or sales roles that produce billable output, making it possible to measure the actual income employees or workgroups generate for the organization. The discussion of utility analysis in Chap. 9 will further probe the quantification of employee outputs in terms of economic benefits for the firm and give attention to the related economic concept of marginal product.

A potential disadvantage specific to the Flamholtz model is the number of subjective assumptions required to estimate future employee outputs. The projected income stream related to employee outputs is modeled as a function of many individual level (e.g., motivation) and organizational level (e.g., opportunity) variables that are difficult to gauge and trend out over time with accuracy. However, some of these factors are aligned with the more recent strategic human capital emphasis on the structural value of the assembled workforce described above. Altogether, the fine-grained adjustments in this case are a conceptual strength but, at the same time, an operational weakness of the technique.

5.5   Capitalized Excess Earnings Method

The capitalized excess earnings method was first promoted by the Department of the United States Treasury in the 1920s as a way to identify intangible asset value, specifically goodwill, embedded within business operations. The basic premise of this approach is that any earnings generated by a business that exceeds a fair rate of return on net tangible assets represent earnings that are attributable to intangible assets. Capitalization of these "excess" earnings therefore provides a value estimate for the intangible assets of a business, which when added to the tangible asset value equates to total business value.

The capitalized excess earnings method is still a commonly used approach, although it has fallen out of favor for income tax purposes and is considered unreliable by some valuation experts. With some additional adjustments to earnings for the non-workforce intangible assets, it is possible to extend this approach to the valuation of the assembled workforce.[5] Below we will consider the steps involved to conduct such an analysis.

- The first stage in the excess earnings analysis is to identify the total normalized annual earnings for the organization. Normalized earnings are simply earnings adjusted to remove the effects of unusual or nonrecurring revenue and expenses.
- Next, calculate the value of net tangible assets. The value of tangible business assets is derived from the financial statements and adjusted to fair value as needed. These assets include cash, inventory, land, buildings and equipment, accounts receivable, and potentially other fixed assets—physical assets that are purchased for long-term use. Deduct accounts payable and other current liabilities from the total value of tangible business assets to determine net value.
- Multiply the net tangible asset value by a reasonable, market-appropriate rate of return to calculate the earnings attributable to the organization's tangible assets. For example, if net tangible asset value totals $2 million and an appropriate rate of return is 10%, earnings attributable to the organization's tangible assets equals $200,000 ($2000,000 × 0.10 = $200,000).
- Subtract the earnings attributed to the organization's tangible assets from the organization's total normalized earnings for the same period to determine excess earnings—the amount of earnings attributable to the intangible business assets. Continuing with the example provided directly above, if annual normalized earnings totaled $500,000, excess earnings equals $300,000 ($500,000 − $200,000 = $300,000).

- To narrow the excess earnings to the amount attributable to the assembled workforce, subtract the earnings derived from any other intangible assets such as patents, royalties, licensing fees, and earnings attributed to intangible assets such as brand name and customer relationships. The remainder is a reasonable estimate of earnings attributable to the assembled workforce. For example, if earnings from other intangible assets were estimated at $100,000, a remainder of $200,000 in earnings would be allocated to the workforce ($300,000 total excess earnings − $100,000 earnings from other intangible assets = $200,000 excess earnings attributed to the workforce).
- Determine the value of the assembled workforce by capitalizing the excess earnings attributed to the workforce. This is done by dividing earnings by an appropriate capitalization rate. In the present example, we will assume a capitalization rate of 15%. Given the above $200,000 in excess earnings attributed to the assembled workforce, a value of $1333,333 is indicated for the workforce ($200,000/0.15 = $1333,333).

Since the capitalization process assumes the income stream is received in perpetuity, the value derived through the excess earnings method is in keeping with the concept of the assembled workforce having an indefinite useful life. The costs to replenish the assembled workforce are presumably reflected in the costs deducted to derive earnings. A key advantage of the excess earnings method is that it is an intuitive and relatively easy method to apply.

There are also several noted limitations of the excess earnings approach. It represents an artificial divide of the company's earnings since the tangible and intangible assets work in interaction to generate earnings. However, this limitation is true of any attempt to allocate a separate value to the assembled workforce. A bigger issue is the difficulty in determining an appropriate capitalization rate for the excess earnings. Since the bulk of intangible assets are not sold apart from the business as a whole, there is little market data to support the reasonableness of capitalization rates for excess earnings.

There are additional limitations to consider when extending the technique to the valuation of the assembled workforce in particular. The appropriateness of the capitalization rate is again hard to determine and subjective. The level of normalized earnings to consider is also subjective. If attempting to include expenses for ongoing replenishment of the workforce, which is conceptually appropriate in order to assume an indefinite asset life, a reserve allowance or an ongoing incremental cost for turnover, training, and lost productivity should be included. Finally, the excess earnings attributable to the assembled workforce run the risk of overstatement if all other intangible assets are not fully deducted from earnings to derive the residual for the workforce. This presents another area of subjectivity in assessing earnings for difficult to quantify intangible assets.

It is also important to consider the level of earnings used in the analysis. Earnings are commonly defined as after-tax income; however, market capitalization rates are typically calculated using net operating income (income before taxes, interest, depreciation, and amortization). Consistency and transparency in the definition of income used at each stage of analysis and among each external comparison is critical in order to avoid misleading value conclusions. Despite the many limitations of the excess earnings approach to valuation of the assembled workforce, it is useful as a reasonableness check against other approaches to valuing the workforce.

5.6   RECONCILING THE INCOME AND COST APPROACH VALUES

The income approach does not generally consider the initial investment (the sunk costs) to assemble the workforce. The income approach is instead a forward-looking view of human capital value. The cost approach, on the other hand, focuses solely on the initial investment to assemble the workforce. As discussed in the previous cost approach section of the book, this is why some have considered the cost approach to represent only the investment in human capital and not the overall economic value of human capital. However, legal precedent suggests the cost approach is the preferred method to valuation of the assembled workforce and the basic economic principle of substitution suggests a reasonable investor would not pay more for an asset than the cost to acquire or build an equivalent substitute. Taken together, it would seem the cost approach sets the value ceiling for the assembled workforce. One way to reconcile the cost and income approach values would therefore be to simply use the income approach value as a check of reasonableness, as a way to substantiate the value determined by the cost approach.

The reasonableness check is a way to reconcile the different values derived through the cost and income approaches to value, but it does not conceptually reconcile the varied views of the assembled workforce presented above. For instance, most of the income approach techniques do not consider the cost of compensation in deriving human capital value. The excess earnings method is a notable exception to this trend. If we were to think conceptually in terms of *net* value of the assembled workforce, the various income approach techniques could be construed as more comparable—to each other and to the cost approach—in their value assumptions.

For instance, a net value via the income approach would offset future employee contributions to firm value by the compensation paid to the same employees in order to derive a net cash flow, which would then be discounted to present value. In the case of the Lev and Schwartz model, the employee contribution to the organization is set as equivalent to employee compensation, so conceptually the net cash flow would be 0. The conceptually justifiable value in this case would simply remain as the cost to assemble the workforce. If you find the conceptual intricacies of the income approach to the valuation of the assembled workforce too ambiguous to follow, you are not alone. The professional, governmental, and academic communities have not come to definitive terms with these issues either. Nonetheless, aspects of the income approach, such as the Lev and Schwartz model's inherent value of employees by skill categorization and remaining years of service, provide a good reference of value for internal decision-making.

5.6.1   Critical Thinking Questions

1. Consider the point made earlier in this chapter that the value of the assembled workforce via the cost approach represents the value ceiling—that is, the most that this asset can be worth based on the economic principle of substitution. Could you make a competing argument for the income approach to value? Would the assembled workforce be worth no greater an amount than the value justified by the present value of the anticipated income it generates for the organization? Is there reason to simply consider the lowest value derived between the cost and income approaches as the ceiling of value?

2. Given the many subjective assumptions that must be made for a discounted cash flow approach to valuing human capital, is direct capitalization always the better choice when valuing the assembled workforce via the income approach?

3. Two of the models described in this chapter value human capital via analysis of the individual employees currently in place. This permits a specific value for each individual employee, assuming sufficient analytical information is available. Does the notion of placing a value on individual employees seem less socially acceptable than valuing the aggregated workforce as an indivisible asset? Or are both approaches simply an accounting and valuation exercise with no symbolic message for how organizations view the human aspect of work?

NOTES

1. Hamermesh, D. S. (1986). The demand for labor in the long run. In O. Ashenfelter and R. Layard (Eds.), *Handbook of Labor Economics, 1*, (pp. 429–471). Cambridge, MA: Elsevier Science Publishers.

2. Lev, B., & Schwartz, A. (1971). On the use of the economic concept of human capital in financial statements. *The Accounting Review, 46*(1), 103–112.

3. Flamholtz, E. G. (1999). *Human resource accounting: Advances in concepts, methods and applications,* 3rd ed. Norwell, MA: Kluwer Academic Publishers.

4. Chadwick, C. (in press). Towards a more comprehensive mode of firms' human capital rents. *Academy of Management Review.* doi:10.5465/ amr.2013.0385.

5. Brummet, R. L., Flamholtz, E. G., & Pyle, W. C. (1968). Human resource measurement–A challenge for accountants. *The Accounting Review, 43*(2), 217–224.

CHAPTER 6

Market Approach to Value

Abstract This chapter examines the market approach to value, also known as the sales comparison approach. The market approach determines the value of an asset based on the selling price of comparable assets, in keeping with the economic principle of substitution. This chapter discusses the conceptual logic of the market approach and reviews three potentially acceptable ways to value the assembled workforce through the market approach. The primary method reviewed is the residual market value technique, which allocates the acquisition price of a business to its different components. The two additional techniques considered are a value extraction method that compares sales that are similar in substantive ways with the exception of the assembled workforce in place, and the direct sale of an assembled workforce by itself.

Keywords Market approach to human capital value · Sales comparison approach to human capital value · Residual value method for human capital value · Sale of assembled workforce

6.1 Conceptual Logic of the Market Approach

The market approach to value, also known as the sales comparison approach, shares a theoretical underpinning with the cost approach in that both are based on the economic principle of substitution, that a rational person would not pay more for an asset than the cost to create

© The Author(s) 2017
K.K. Merriman, *Valuation of Human Capital*,
DOI 10.1007/978-3-319-58934-3_6

or acquire a substitute of comparable utility. The market approach also relies on the economic principles of competition and equilibrium, which suggest that in a free market where the flow of information and transactions between buyers and sellers is unrestricted, a market "equilibrium" price will emerge that brings demand and supply into balance. More specifically, a market approach determines the value of an asset based on the selling price of comparable assets, or in the case of an intangible asset like human capital that is an integral part of a larger asset, the portion of the overall selling price that the integral asset is estimated to represent.

Applying the market approach to the valuation of the assembled workforce is challenging because people are generally not owned and sold, therefore a directly identifiable market value of individuals is not common. *Employment contracts* are owned and may be transferred, and this is particularly common with professional athletes. However, since the abolition of slavery, individuals are not owned assets in the traditional since. Human assets are not controlled by the organization beyond the basic transactional exchange of services for pay. Human capital resides within and is owned by—and ultimately controlled by—the employee. Even when organizations invest in their employees to develop employee human capital, the employer is simply "renting" the use of this human capital via the compensation paid to employees.

Employers may have ways to attempt to protect their *investment* in human capital such as a requirement to pay back tuition reimbursements if an employee leaves the organization within a certain timeframe after receiving the benefit, or non-compete clauses for a duration of time after leaving the organization, or an employment contract for a specific duration of time. However, none of these circumstances indicate ownership of the human asset's full market value. Indeed, this is the issue at the heart of the non-reporting of human capital value for financial reporting and accounting purposes.

Ownership of the assembled workforce as an asset is more easily understood when human capital is viewed in aggregate rather than in terms of individual employees. In keeping with the tax accounting concept of a mass asset, certain types of intangible assets are considered in aggregate as a single entity based on the logic that even though individual components of the asset may terminate at different times, these individual components can be replaced without causing notable fluctuations or losses in value of the asset as a whole. If a company is assumed to continually regenerate the assembled workforce through new hires and training when positions are vacated, then the asset of the assembled workforce as a whole remains materially constant in function even if the individual elements that comprise the asset change over time. Of course, in practice there may be employees that are deemed irreplaceable. It can also take significant ongoing regeneration efforts on the part of a company to preserve a workforce under even the best circumstances. Companies are essentially preserving and creating a new asset simultaneously, though the line between the original and new asset is subtle and continuously shifting. See the legal opinions on the Ithaca Industries case discussed in Chap. 3 for a more thorough discussion of these concepts.[1] Even though the purpose in the Ithaca Industries case for discussing the mass asset concept is not the same as ours, it still provides insights into how to think of companies "owning" their workforce. They liken it to an example of a tangible and more traditionally recognized business asset like a truck, which can be preserved indefinitely through replacement of parts and maintenance. So while many aspects of a firm's human capital are not controlled by the firm—particularly if and when individual employees choose to leave—the firm can still be said to own the value of the aggregate asset of the assembled workforce as a whole.

There is general agreement around three potentially acceptable ways to value the assembled workforce through the market approach. The most common is a residual market value technique in which the acquisition price of a business can be allocated to its different components. Less common is a value extraction technique that compares sales of businesses that are similar in substantive ways with the exception of the assembled workforce in place, though it is not often that a business sells without an assembled workforce. The third and also less common method is sales of an assembled workforce by itself. Though this is of course the most straightforward way to identify the isolated value of the assembled workforce, this type of market transaction is not typical. We will discuss each of these techniques next in more detail.

6.2   RESIDUAL VALUE METHOD

The residual method starts with the value of the overall business. This method is typically used for a newly acquired business, where the overall value is indicated by the acquisition price. When a business is acquired, the acquisition price is often allocated among the assets of the business for accounting purposes. This normally takes place after the acquisition rather than as part of the determination of acquisition price. The separate identification and negotiation of the value of a businesses' workforce at the time of acquisition is rare. Therefore, market data on the sale of businesses does not support a true sales comparison approach for the assembled workforce. The market data is instead an allocated value derived from a series of value estimates pertaining to components of the business assets.

Two terms pertaining to businesses are useful to know in analyzing the components of business value: going concern value and goodwill. Going concern value refers to the additional value that attaches to a company as an ongoing entity, recognizing its ability to continue generating income without interruption despite a change in ownerships. While the term is used rather narrowly for income tax purposes, outside of the tax accounting domain the term often refers to the total value of the operating business. Under this broad conceptualization of the term, goodwill is one component of the going concern value that derives from the intangibles inherent to the business that are not separately identifiable, such as customer relationships and the assembled workforce. Conceptually, goodwill stems from the established business relationships and the expectation that these relationships (with the assembled workforce, customers, suppliers, etc.) may continue indefinitely. Goodwill is quantified as a residual amount—the portion of the acquisition cost over and above the value of the tangible assets and identifiable intangible assets. The excess earnings method described under income approaches to value in Chap. 5 follows this same residual value logic.

As noted above, the assembled workforce is part of goodwill. After the value of goodwill is determined through the residual method, further adjustments are needed to isolate the portion of value under goodwill that is attributable to the assembled workforce. For regulatory financial reporting purposes, the assembled workforce is considered an unidentifiable intangible asset—an asset that is not recognized separately. Therefore, the components of value encompassed within goodwill are not identified on the financial statements. However, the United States income tax accounting regulations allow the "value" attributable to the assembled workforce at the time a company is acquired to be treated as an amortized deduction for income tax purposes, per section 197 of the Internal Revenue Code.[2] These records do break out the assembled workforce as a component of goodwill, although the process or adjustments made to do so is a point of consternation among tax professionals.[3]

Taken together, in theory the residual value attributed to the assembled workforce is determined as follows:

- The total value or acquisition price of the business is established.
- The portion of total business value that exceeds the fair value of tangible net assets (land, building, machinery and equipment, inventory) is allocated to intangible assets
- The portion of value allocated to intangibles that exceeds the fair value of the identified intangible assets of the business (e.g., patents, copyrights, trademarks, trade names, franchise, licenses) is allocated to goodwill
- The portion of value allocated to goodwill is further adjusted to deduct all "non-identified" intangible assets other than the assembled workforce, such as the business reputation, brand, and customer relationships.

Notice that in order to complete this last step, some reliable means of identifying value for these other non-identified intangible assets is needed. Consistent with the International Financial Reporting Standards (IFRS) and the U.S. Generally Accepted Accounting Principles (GAAP), fair value is the value that would result in an arm's length market transaction between buyers and sellers. The assumption is that the best estimate of value is an actual market price. However, in the case of intangible assets, often this type of actual transaction is absent and the next best thing is the use of acceptable methods and reasonable assumptions to estimate a market value.

Due to the many assumptions needed to derive the residual value of the assembled workforce, the residual technique is more a thought exercise than a true market approach to the valuation of human capital. The result is useful for amortizing certain acquisition costs for tax accounting purposes. It is not common or particularly useful though for decision-making purposes by internal and external stakeholders, largely because of the many assumptions required, and also because of the anchoring of the value in one static point in time.

6.3   COMPARATIVE ANALYSIS OF INCREMENTAL
VALUE DIFFERENCES

A less common approach due to its limited occurrence in the market is the comparison across sales of businesses that are similar in substantive ways with the exception of the assembled workforce in place. This approach is referred to as a paired-sales analysis in the real estate appraisal field. It involves extracting the incremental value difference for the component of value of interest. For instance, nursing homes and hotels are good examples of businesses that sometimes sell in a nonoperating state. Even if no longer operating as a going concern, the business has value in the market based on its tangible assets such as the building, furniture, fixtures and equipment, and any potential intangible asset value that may remain in terms of customer lists, reputation, licenses, etc. A comparison between the sales price of such a property with the sales price of a comparable property that is in operation provides an incremental difference in value that may be used to justify the value of an assembled workforce.

Of course, rarely would sales match exactly on all qualities other than the assembled workforce. Therefore, when considering "matched" sales of similar assets, it is necessary to make value adjustments for any differences between the businesses that may drive a difference in the market value, such as business size and location, so that the only difference unaccounted for between the comparable properties is the presence or absence of the assembled workforce.

Once a value for the assembled workforce is extracted, it must be converted to a relevant unit of comparison in order to translate the extrapolated value of the workforce to the business context of interest. Often the initial sales comparison process is conducted based on a unit of comparison rather than in whole numbers, in which case this step will have been accomplished earlier in the process. Unit rates relevant for the valuation of the assembled workforce include average value per employee, proportion of assembled workforce value to total business value, or assembled workforce value expressed as a multiple of income.

6.4   SALE OF ASSEMBLED WORKFORCE

The assembled workforce or a subgroup of the assembled workforce can be viewed as a profit-center group. A profit-center group is a workgroup for which inputs (investments in assembling and training the workgroup) and outputs (revenue generating services provided by the workgroup) are both identifiable in monetary terms. A salesforce is a prime example.

Table 6.1   Example of a workforce sale

Profit-Center Group Massachusetts Mutual Life Insurance acquired MetLife's retail life insurance advisor group, known as Met Life Premier Client Group, in July 2016. The acquisition consisted of an estimated 4000 advisors working across the U.S. in more than 40 locations, forming a distribution channel with advisors serving as intermediaries to retain existing customers and attract new customers

Acquisition Price The recorded acquisition price in this case can be construed as largely driven by the assembled workforce. The adjustments to remove tangible and other intangible businesses assets from the acquisition price are relatively modest and more straightforward compared to an entire organization with an assembled workforce comprised of a diverse set of work groups. A unit rate is derived by dividing the acquisition price by 4000, which is the total number of advisors within the group

---

Flamholtz, a pioneer in the field of human resource accounting, considered the valuation of profit-center groups via their relative economic contribution to the overall economic value of the firm.[4] Calculation of total firm value involves discounting projected future earnings to present value, an income approach method discussed in Chap. 5. The relative amount then attributable to the group of employees, as a single profit-center group, can be based on the ratio of investment in human resources (e.g., the replacement cost) relative to total investment in resources. This approach is reportedly common in the insurance industry to value insurance agents in aggregate when insurance firms transfer ownership.

Two things should be apparent to the reader regarding this method. First, this is primarily an income approach to value. Second, it is an approach that requires a number of assumptions, particularly surrounding projections of uncertain future income, and is therefore a more speculative measure of human capital value. However, on somewhat rare occasions, a profit-center group may be acquired separately from the larger business as a whole. Events such as this can provide a more direct indication of value for the assembled workforce. An example of such an event is described in Table 6.1.

6.5   ADVANTAGES AND DISADVANTAGES OF THE MARKET APPROACH

A key advantage of the market approach is it actually represents what market participants have been willing to pay for the asset in question. The disadvantage in applying the market approach to the valuation of the assembled workforce is there is not an organized or active market for this standalone asset. Instead, a firm's aggregate human capital tends to transfer as an integral part of the overall business. However, the different methods described here—residual value method, comparative analysis of incremental value differences, and the infrequent sales of an assembled workforce—provide ways to conceptually think about the value of human capital, even when a precise number is not feasible to derive.

6.5.1   Critical Thinking Questions

1. Start-up companies, especially in the technology sector, are sometimes purchased solely or primarily because of the inherent value in the assembled workgroup and other knowledge assets within the business. Contrast this approach with assembling the workforce instead of acquiring it already assembled. Use your knowledge from the cost approach chapters to inform your reflection. When and why would acquisition of the assembled workforce be potentially a more efficient and strategic way to proceed?

2. The market approach to value is a dominant approach in the valuation of certain types of real estate and other tangible assets that sell relatively frequently. Market transactions also inform the income approach by providing a source for market-based capitalization rates. The importance of market transactions is that they reflect the *actual behaviors* of buyers and sellers—rather than simply estimates based on hypotheticals. Yet the market approach is the weakest approach for the valuation of the assembled workforce. Discuss why. Also consider how the cost approach to value reflects actual market-type behaviors for the valuation of the assembled workforce.

3. This chapter described the assembled workforce also as part of goodwill value. If the acquisition price of a business does not exceed its net tangible asset value—i.e., goodwill is zero—does the assembled workforce have no value? Relate this point to the descriptions of depreciation and obsolescence from the cost approach chapters.

NOTES

1. Ithaca Industries, Inc., Appellant, v. Commissioner of Internal Revenue, Appellee, 17 F.3d 684 (4th Cir. 1994). Retrieved from http://law.justia. com/cases/federal/appellate-courts/F3/17/684/566900/ and http://

www.allcourtdata.com/law/case/ithaca-industries-inc-v-commissioner-of-internal-revenue/cA5xdj8?page=1.
2. Legal Information Institute, Cornell University. 26 CFR 1.197–2—Amortization of goodwill and certain other intangibles. Retrieved from https://www.law.cornell.edu/cfr/text/26/1.197-2.
3. Weiss, R. (2009, January). Fifteen years of antichurning: It's time to make butter. *Tax Notes*. Retrieved from http://www.gibsondunn.com/publications/Documents/Weiss-Antichurning.pdf.
4. See pp. 193–194 Flamholtz, E. G. (1999). *Human resource accounting: Advances in concepts, methods and applications*, 3rd ed. Norwell, MA: Kluwer Academic Publishers.

CHAPTER 7

Sustaining Human Capital Value

Abstract This chapter examines a basic but essential premise underlying the value of the assembled workforce. That is, for the workforce to have an ongoing value, its value producing properties must be sustained. The ongoing value of the assembled workforce is dependent on how the human resources are developed, trained, and employed going forward to maintain, enhance, or deplete the aggregate human capital value. This chapter draws from a range of research literature to describe four areas in which employer investment in employees is shown to impact employee performance contributions over the long-term: regeneration of physical and mental health, regeneration of viable skills, and maintenance of motivation.

Keywords Sustaining human capital · Performance-regeneration paradox · Human welfare

7.1 SUSTAINING THE HUMAN "ASSET"

Under current accounting standards and thinking, the human resource of a firm is treated as a cost (compensation) charged against revenue. There is no separately recorded asset on the balance sheet for human resources, though long-term liabilities associated with human resources, such as pensions, are recorded. The contemporary thinking, though financial accounting standards have not caught up to this point, is that

© The Author(s) 2017
K.K. Merriman, *Valuation of Human Capital*,
DOI 10.1007/978-3-319-58934-3_7

the firm's human resources are in place to logically render not just current services, but also to provide future services that can be translated into an estimate of present economic value. Implicit in this point is that hiring and training costs are more appropriately viewed as an investment toward future revenue rather than simply as costs against current revenue—similar to other forms of capital investments by organizations.

Importantly, the view described above relies on a basic but essential premise: for the workforce to have an ongoing value, its value producing properties must be sustained. The ongoing value of the assembled workforce is dependent on how the human resources are developed, trained, and employed going forward to maintain, enhance or deplete the aggregate human capital value. For example, will the human capital of the workforce suffer from functional obsolescence or will functional utility remain viable or even be enhanced? Will employee turnover impair the value of the assembled workforce or will turnover remain at a functional level with departing employees replaced in an equivalent-utility fashion?

The replacement cost of human capital considers the value at one point in time, after a workforce is assembled and at a stabilized level of performance. Existing deficiencies in the composition and skill set of the assembled workforces are reflected in deductions for depreciation. However, the notion of depreciation can also be viewed proactively in the form of actions needed to sustain the value of a firm's human capital. Research points to four key areas in which employer investment in employees is shown to impact employee performance contributions over the long-term: regeneration of physical and mental health, regeneration of viable skills, and maintenance of motivation. Each of these areas is described in more detail throughout this chapter.

7.2   The Performance-Regeneration Paradox

The regeneration of employee physical and mental health is best understood through the lens of the performance-regeneration paradox. The relationship between work hours and human capital is curvilinear. That is, productivity increases in relation to work hours to a point, but there is a subjective threshold at which the number of hours worked begins to erode rather than enhance human capital.[1]

This phenomenon is labeled the performance-regeneration paradox because the more time and energy employees devote to increased work performance and productivity, the less time and energy they have available for regeneration of the qualities needed to sustain work performance and productivity.[2] Said another way, lack of regeneration equates to a higher rate of depreciation and obsolescence for the human capital embodied by the assembled workforce. To sustain the performance ability of the firm's human resources, human resource consumption (e.g., high-performance demands) must be balanced with resource regeneration in the form of maintenance of employee physical and mental health and viable skills.

Though long-term individual input of many work hours has well-documented negative effects on mental and physical health[3], the implications for maintenance of knowledge and skills are less straightforward. On-the-job learning and job specialization may be enhanced by the number of hours worked.[4] But a dynamic, changing environment requires ongoing learning beyond immediate job duties. If this type of learning must take place off the clock, the opportunity cost may lead to deferred or overly efficient (i.e., seeking the least that will do) investment of time and effort in new knowledge on the part of employees.

Even when learning takes place on the job or during work hours, working too many hours may still have deleterious effects for the absorption or application of new knowledge. For instance, a study of medical interns training at teaching hospitals found that the interns made a significantly greater number of serious medical, medication, and diagnostic errors when working traditionally long hours versus reduced hours.[5] Though medical interns represent an extreme example, the basic principle generalizes to other types of workers. Specifically, this suggests that employee learning, along with physical and mental health, erodes when work consistently encompasses too many hours.

Organizations can address this issue by proactively limiting hours worked and requiring regular time off, especially for high achieving employees that embrace long discretionary work hours. Formal policies and enforcement efforts on the part of employers are needed since high achieving employees may be unaware or ignore the deteriorating effects of overwork when striving to get ahead.[6] For instance, in a study of hardworking management consultants, business consulting teams experienced performance gains when their members were *required* to take regular time off from their otherwise long work hours.[7]

7.3   Financial Investment in Ongoing Learning

In addition to ensuring time for employee regeneration, which is essentially an indirect facilitation of employee maintenance of knowledge and skills, companies must directly invest in employees' ongoing learning to assure sustainable human capital—prevent depreciation of human capital value—and potentially increase human capital value. This point is supported by a study that examined the degree of direct education and training investments at the firm level in relation to subsequent year financial measures using a sample of 575 publicly traded U.S. firms. The study findings showed a significant return on investment from training.[8]

The authors of the above study noted that training expenditures reduce income but are not reported to investors in specific terms, and therefore the potential upward influence on future company performance is not reflected in current share values. Thus subsequent year share value and dividends were expected to be greater for these essentially undervalued firms relative to firms without the hidden investment and upside potential in employee training. Controlling for extraneous factors such as industry, prior firm performance, firm size, and more, the study did indeed find that organizations in the top half in terms of training expenditures had a significantly greater total average stock return (dividends and share value increase = 36.9%) than companies in the lower half of training expenditures (19.8%) and the S&P 500 for the same timeframe (25.5%). Though the data used for this study ranged from 1996 to 1999, the relationship should be similar or greater today given the knowledge economy.[9]

Despite the stated imperative regarding ongoing learning, there are certainly rational reasons why organizations may hesitate to invest in employee training. Organizational investments in employee training represent a current business expense when training occurs, but can take time to translate into performance and productivity gains. Further, investments in training are relatively risky compared to investments in physical assets or intangibles such as patents that the company actually owns. Employees are not owned and may generally leave an organization at will and take the benefits of the training investment with them.

However, when the value of the assembled workforce is quantified, it makes salient the otherwise hidden cost or loss of value that occurs when the firm's human capital is not maintained. Further, with the growth in self-directed training modules facilitated online, and with large providers such as Coursera and LinkedIn offering modules across an extensive range of competencies, the cost of training is greatly reduced. Organizations need only, in some cases, to provide the incentives and time for employees to pursue relevant training opportunities.

7.4 EMPLOYEE MOTIVATION

Maintenance of employees' skills and competencies, as described so far in this chapter, is a necessary but insufficient condition for maintaining work productivity and the value of the assembled workforce. Employees may possess the upmost talent and knowledge to do the job—i.e., the capacity to do the job, but fall short of expectations if they lack the motivation to apply their human capital to the task at hand. Conversely, a less qualified employee may exceed expectations when highly motivated to perform.

Organizations that give attention to the important aspect of employee motivation tend to focus on the quantity aspect of motivation. The general idea is that more motivation is better. When motivation is viewed in terms of quantity, we are generally speaking of extrinsic motivation. Workplace factors that contribute to extrinsic motivation include fair pay, feedback, recognition, opportunities for advancement, and other desirable outcomes that are bestowed on employees by the organization.

In addition to the quantity of motivation, however, equally important is the *quality* of motivation. Self-determination theory distinguishes qualitative differences in extrinsic motivation based on the degree to which individuals have internalized motivation.[10] Extrinsic motivation is said to range from completely externally controlled (e.g., performing work tasks primarily to gain reward or avoid punishment) through fully internalized based on individuals' identification with their work role (e.g., performing work tasks because the behavior is integrated with one's sense of self).

A productive degree of internalization of motivation occurs when people identify with the value of a behavior for their own self-selected goals; in turn, people feel their behavior is relatively self-determined since it is more congruent with their personal goals and identities.[11] Research on this topic suggests that self-determination represents a fundamental human need, and a need individuals are driven to fulfill. Similarly, individuals inherently ascribe broad purposes to their work and experience meaningfulness when the work context is perceived to be in concordance with these self-determined purposes. In turn, this experienced meaningfulness is thought to lead to a greater degree of dedication and absorption in one's work role.[12]

Therefore, in order to optimize the human capital of the assembled workforce, organizations must go beyond addressing extrinsic motivation and attempt to understand, encourage, and support the broader purpose employees ascribe to their work. A *Harvard Business Review* article titled "Finding Meaning at Work, Even When Your Job Is Dull" provides some particularly good research-based examples of how employers can effectively accomplish this.[13] Offering employees opportunities to learn is one way suggested to enhance meaning, and this also happens to address the earlier described need for ongoing learning. The resulting benefit for the organization is an internalized level of motivation among employees that not only inspires high levels of performance, but also supplants the need for monitoring and external control of employees.

7.5   HUMAN WELFARE AS A GOAL ITSELF

It is important to emphasize that, separate from the potential impacts on the firm's human capital, employee welfare is a fundamental and intrinsically worthy outcome on its own. A humanistic perspective of management places human welfare as the overarching business outcome of interest. Under the humanistic paradigm, the notion that employee welfare also supports economic value is incidental to justification of the former's pursuit.

For instance, esteemed organizational scholar Jeffrey Pfeffer contends that research, public policy, and business practice alike must set aside the ubiquitous economic lens that overshadows concerns for human well-being.[14] Readers may also learn more about the humanistic paradigm through perusing the materials available at the Humanist Management Network website (http://www.humanetwork.org/), a nonprofit group devoted to furthering education and practice in this area. You will find a number of research studies and resources available on this site.

The normative or moral argument for business to support human welfare is not inconsistent with the economic argument for sustainable human capital value. In fact, the economic argument outlined in this chapter may bolster attention to the human welfare imperative. Providing the logic and empirical support to clearly link employee-welfare-related outcomes (regeneration, learning, self-determined motivation) to the firm's economic-related outcomes (human capital performance and productivity) provides a business incentive to support employee welfare. The synergy between the human and economic perspectives in this case is supported when the *sustainability* of human capital value *over time* is emphasized, versus its short-term value at a static point in time.

7.5.1 Critical Thinking Questions

1. Reflect on a time when you perceived your work as aligned with your broader goals and life purpose. Now reflect on a time when you were working strictly for the money. In which context did you feel most driven to perform at a high level?
2. Organizations that allow employees to receive additional pay in lieu of paid time off may inadvertently reduce employee productivity over time. Drawing on the information discussed in this chapter, explain why this otherwise seemingly fair incentive could have an undesirable effect on employee productivity in the long run.
3. Many professions, ranging from financial professionals to medical workers, require continuing education to maintain professional licenses and certifications. Why is mandatory and even voluntary continuing education more prevalent in some fields than others? Are there any fields where ongoing learning of some sort is not a concern at all, where the knowledge an employee has at time of hire is sufficient to do the job in perpetuity?

Notes

1. Merriman, K. K. (2014). The psychological role of pay systems in choosing to work more hours. *Human Resource Management Review, 24,* 67–79.
2. Ehnert, I. (2009). *Sustainable human resource management: A conceptual and exploratory analysis from a paradox perspective.* New York: Springer.
3. Kivimäki, M., Batty, G. D., Hamer, M., Ferrie, J. E., Vahtera, J., Virtanen, M., et al. (2011). Using additional information on working hours to predict coronary heart disease: A cohort study. *Annals of Internal Medicine, 154,* 457–463. Also see Virtanen, M., Ferrie, J. E., Singh-Manoux, A., Shipley, M. J., Stansfeld, S. A., Marmot, M. G., et al. (2011). Long working hours and symptoms of anxiety and depression: A 5 year follow up of the Whitehall II study. *Psychological Medicine.* 10.1017/S0033291711000171.

4. Barzel, Y., & Yu, B. T. (1984). The effect of the utilization rate on the division of labor. *Economic Inquiry, 22,* 18–27.
5. Landrigan, C. P., Rothschild, J. M., Cronin, J. W., Kaushal, R., Burdick, E., Katz, J. T., et al. (2004). Effect of reducing interns' work hours on serious medical errors in intensive care units. *The New England Journal of Medicine, 351,* 1838–1848.
6. Ryvkin, D. (2011). Fatigue in dynamic tournaments. *Journal of Economics and Management Strategy, 20,* 1011–1041.
7. Perlow, L. A., & Porter, J. L. (2009). Making time off predictable—and required. *Harvard Business Review, 87,* 102–109.
8. Bassi, L. J., Ludwig, J., McMurrer, D. P., & Van Buren, M. (2002). Profiting from learning: Firm-level effects of training investments and market implications. *Singapore Management Review, 24*(3), 61–76.
9. Ibid.
10. Deci E. L., & Ryan R. M (2000). The 'what' and 'why' of goal pursuits: Human needs and the self-determination of behavior. *Psychological Inquiry, 11*(4), 227–268.
11. Gagné M., & Deci E. L (2005). Self-determination theory and work motivation. *Journal of Organizational Behavior, 26*(4), 331–362.
12. Barrick M. R., Mount M. K., & Li N. (2013). The theory of purposeful work behavior: The role of personality, higher-order goals, and job characteristics. *Academy of Management Review 38*(1), 132–153.
13. Hansen, M., & Keltner, D. (2012). Finding meaning at work, even when your job is dull. *Harvard Business Review Online, December, 20.* Retrieved from https://hbr.org/2012/12/finding-meaning-at-work-even-w.
14. Pfeffer, J. (2016). Why the assholes are winning: Money trumps all. *Journal of Management Studies.* doi:10.1111/joms.12177.

CHAPTER 8

Leveraging Human Capital via Organizational Social Capital

Abstract This chapter examines organizational social capital, an intangible asset embedded in the quality of the relationships among organizational members. Organizational social capital emphasizes the interconnections between the people that comprise the assembled workforce. It is thought to generate "relational wealth" for an organization by facilitating individual employee commitment to the collective good. This chapter defines and distinguishes the organization's social capital from its human capital, and discusses research on how social capital enhances the value of the assembled workforce. Also considered are ways organizations can develop social capital and the potential detractions to social capital value.

Keywords Organizational social capital · Social capital value Relational wealth · Workplace reciprocity

8.1 Defining Organizational Social Capital

In addition to a firm's physical, financial, and human capitals, there is its social capital, an intangible factor rooted in the quality of the organization's relationships, and providing a difficult to imitate competitive advantage.[1] Social capital generates "relational wealth" for an organization by justifying individual employee commitment to the collective good and thus serving to manage collective action, among other benefits.[2]

© The Author(s) 2017
K.K. Merriman, *Valuation of Human Capital*,
DOI 10.1007/978-3-319-58934-3_8

Organizational social capital is defined as "a resource reflecting the character of social relations within the organization, realized through members' levels of collective goal orientation and shared trust."[3] Organizational social capital is a relatively recent construct compared to the precursors of social capital in other domains. In their 1999 publication, scholars Leana and Van Buren drew from the broader, well-established literature on social capital in societal and individual domains to construe the above definition for the dimension of social capital that resides specifically within the organization. Their view positions social capital as an attribute of the organization that exists among its organizational members.

8.2   DISTINGUISHING ORGANIZATIONAL SOCIAL CAPITAL FROM HUMAN CAPITAL

To clarify the distinction between social and human capitals, it is first necessary to have a fuller understanding of how social capital and its associated value are derived. *Social capital in general*, the broader aspects of social capital beyond the organization, stems from the concept that social networks contribute to efficient facilitation of actions. Said simply, there is value in all forms of social networks. This value—i.e., social capital—emerges from connections between individuals and resides within the social relations and networks of the particular social network in question. Therefore, social capital is described as having a structural, relational, and cognitive aspect. It entails the structural linking of group members to channels of social interaction and includes the quantity and quality of the network links.

Social capital is also influenced by relational aspects of the group, particularly mutual trust, and a shared cognitive understanding among group members with regards to norms, values, attitudes, and beliefs. These are the aspects that are particularly relevant to *organizational* social capital. Whereas the quantity and type of connections within a social network are emphasized in some areas of social capital research, organizational social capital emphasizes the cooperative quality of the interactions for collective goal accomplishment.

With this basic understanding of social capital value, we can now turn to distinguishing organizational social capital from human capital. Whereas human capital resides within the individual employee, although organizations may contribute and benefit from it, organizational social capital is a quality of the social relations within the firm and can be considered an attribute of the organization even if not singularly owned in the same sense as financial and physical assets. Some scholars extend the concept of organizational social capital to include employees' individual networks outside the firm, though this individualized level of social capital goes beyond what we would conceive as an asset of the organization. Similarly, by some definitions, the organization's social capital with external stakeholders can encompass relationships with suppliers, customers, investors, and others, but the value of these external relationships is outside the scope of value attributed to the assembled workforce.

Organizational social capital includes all members of the organization, but does not rely on any one individual. Its value instead relies on the social unit, and individuals within the social unit are potentially replaceable without eroding the overall embedded social capital. The thinking is that once the norms and values that support social capital are firmly embedded within the organization's members and broader culture, new employees can be socialized into the system without significant disruption.

8.3   How Organizational Social Capital Enhances Human Capital Value

Some extent of social capital is needed in all organizations to assure that human capital represented by each individual employee is, in aggregate, worth at least the sum of its parts and potentially more. Collective organizational goals that require interdependent human capital cannot be accomplished if employees are not able or willing to work interdependently. Interdependency is more the norm than exception in contemporary work environments. When we talk about the value of the firm's human capital, we refer to the full assembled workforce. Social capital emphasizes the interconnections between the people that comprise the assembled workforce.

It creates value through facilitating collective action. Organizational social capital reflects the willingness of individual employees to subordinate their own self-interests and individual goals to the collective goals and actions necessary for organizational goal achievement when self and collective interests are not otherwise perfectly aligned. It is "taking one for the team" when needed. Without such cooperation, the individuals that comprise the organization's workforce are more susceptible to power struggles, conflicting goals, limited knowledge sharing, an unwillingness to go beyond prescribed job duties and other individualistic tendencies. Organizational social capital greases the wheels for interconnected actions among employees. As management guru Edwards Deming observed many years ago, it takes teamwork to accomplish organizational goals, just as the performance of an orchestra depends on how players work together more so than the talent of any single performer.

Quantifying the added value of social capital in terms of worker outputs is difficult. A relatively rare and interesting field experiment involving workers at a UK fruit farm provides some empirical support.[4] The experiment involved workers hired on seasonal contracts ranging from 2 to 6 months, and consisted of university students drawn from ten different Eastern European countries. These conditions permitted potential wide variation in social ties among subgroups of workers due to differences in language, differences in work start dates, and differences in physical proximity among workers. Various cohorts of workers were observed over 2 years. Despite the short-term nature of the work, the researchers found that worker productivity, defined as the kilograms of fruit picked, was enhanced by 17% through social capital—i.e., when the same worker was managed by individuals he was socially connected to versus different days when the worker was managed by individuals he was not socially connected to. It should also be noted that all managers were paid a fixed wage and all workers were paid the same piece rate for their labor, thus the interesting results were not confounded by financial incentive differences.

But why do workers produce more in the presence of organizational social capital? While the broader literature on social capital in its most general form construes it as either a public or an individual asset, the benefits of organizational social capital accrue to the organization *and* its members. In fact, in order for organizational social capital to sustain, members must ultimately perceive a benefit to themselves as an incentive to contribute to organizational social capital. Individual benefits may take the form of compensation enhancements and intrinsically valued outcomes such as a sense of belongingness and competence, and are more typically indirect and distant rather than direct and current. Rationally speaking though, the stronger the perceived self-benefit, the more motivated members are to engage in acts to enhance social capital. Compensation systems that reward team goals or that recognize individuals based on their contributions to the collective goals of the organization provide one obvious benefit for employees that adopt a collective goal orientation. But reward systems are notoriously tricky in this regard since it is often difficult to determine who has meaningfully contributed to collective outcomes.

Thus integral to the perceived benefit for individuals is mutual trust among members—e.g., trust among members that their efforts will be reciprocated, that other members are not prone to social loafing, and trust in the broader norms and behaviors of the social unit as a whole (the organization) that all members will contribute to social capital and ultimately share in the collective benefits stemming from social capital without need for one-on-one quid pro quo. In this way, a new member of the group does not specifically need to earn individual trust, but is instead an immediate contributor to and beneficiary of the group's social capital simply by group association and implicit acceptance of the group's norms. Therefore, once established, social capital and the resulting cohesion of the group in their collective action toward group goals is a durable organizational asset that is not necessarily eroded by the removal or addition of organizational members.

8.4 Ways Firms Develop Organizational Social Capital

Employment practices, and particularly the human resource management practices of an organization as discussed below, are considered instrumental in facilitating social capital within organizations. They are a primary means by which social capital is shaped and value is extracted and realized for the firm and its employees. Thus, unlike human capital that is owned by each individual employee, social capital is to a large degree inherent in the employment practices of the firm that create, guide, and maintain the social relations within the firm.

In keeping with the notion that firms permit and encourage social capital through employment practices, Leana and Van Buren, in their 1999 seminal model, posed three ways that social capital may be built and maintained through employment practices:

1. Stable relationships among organizational members
2. Organizational reciprocity norms
3. Specified roles reinforced by bureaucratic procedures.

Stable employment relationships are a foundation for reciprocity and allow time for meaningful and trusting relationships to develop between coworkers and between employees and the organization. Reciprocity norms refer to an informal but embedded aspect of organizational standards and culture that adheres to the universal principles of social exchange in which individuals feel a sense of social obligation to repay beneficial acts received from others—to return the favor. The expectation of beneficial reciprocity is weaker or absent altogether in work environments that are highly competitive. For example, compensation systems that ignore collective goals and group member contributions and that overly emphasize individual achievement potentially undermine the development of social capital. Beneficial reciprocity is also lacking in employment relationships that are purely transactional in nature with no expectation beyond the exchange of specified work for specified pay. Conversely, employment relationships are deemed more relational and thus supportive of social capital when employers offer job benefits that emphasize a long-term relationship, such as investment in employee development, training, well-being, and job security. The scholarly work of Denise Rousseau provides seminal and subsequent insights into the formation and qualities of relational versus transactional exchange relationships between employees and employers.[5]

In the absence of stable relationships and internalized common values among employees that foster social capital, formal organizational procedures, policies, and job-role specifications can establish explicit protocol that facilitates, to some degree, the benefits of social capital. That is, aspects such as informal networks, mutual trust, and shared identity that develop between people over time in stable relationships can be replaced with bureaucratic structure that does not rely on relationship quality to encourage collective action toward collective goals. The emphasis on relationships is substituted with an emphasis on job roles and compliance to role requirements that specify interdependence. However, establishing sufficient formal networks and rules for collective action, and monitoring employee compliance bring about its own set of complexities and costs since not all forms of collective actions can be foreseen as needed and specified in advance, nor easily monitored for compliance. This inefficiency in imposed collective action is perhaps largest when it comes to knowledge sharing among employees. It is difficult to require that employees share good ideas or other discretionary resources with each other, or for organizations to even know when full knowledge has been withheld for individualistic reasons that put self-interest above the collective goals.

8.5 DETRACTIONS FROM SOCIAL CAPITAL VALUE

Organizational social capital includes all members of the organization—full-time and part-time employees, regular and contingent workers. However, just as the cost approach to value of the assembled workforce conceptually and empirically relies on a degree of stability among the employees, so does the value of social capital stemming from the assembled workforce. Contingent and temporary employees certainly provide value to firms in many ways, for example, as a means to flexibly grow and shrink the workforce and tap into a unique skill set that is only temporarily needed. But this value resides more firmly within the operating business and does not extend to the value ascribed to the assembled workforce, particular under the cost approach to valuing human capital. A primary reason is contingent and temporary workers are assumed to be easily replaced based on the short-term nature of their employment. If a new business owner can easily hire their own set of contingent and temporary workers, there is little reason for them to pay extra for this component of the business during an acquisition.

Of course, as contingent work continues to evolve we can envision exceptions to this view. For example, drivers for ridesharing platforms such as Uber and Lyft are contingent workers, but the stability and loyalty of the contingent workforce undoubtedly contributes value to the business in a similar way as an assembled workforce in a more traditionally structured organization. Perhaps the value inherent in worker relationships for the firm in that case is strictly a social capital value rather than any human capital value. Scholarship and practice must evolve to consider new ways of assembling human capital.

It must also be noted that organizational social capital, despite all of the advantages discussed above, also has the potential to be detrimental to the value of the assembled workforce. Strong ties among employees derived from stability and shared values may, at the same time, create peer pressure among employees to conform to the status quo. It may therefore discourage contrarian, innovative ideas from emerging within the group. The optimal degree of social capital will vary across firms, but in each case there is certainly a point of diminishing and even negative returns to consider. Too little social capital can prohibit needed cooperation among the workforce, whereas too much may result in a workforce that resembles a unified school of fish simply swimming in the same direction for social consistency reasons.

Relatedly, social capital among employees may increase the likelihood of employees leaving the organization en masse as cohesively networked colleagues are recruited collectively or may prefer to follow their colleagues out of the organization due to greater loyalty to their workgroup than to the organization. Speaking to this point, scholars Dess and Shaw caution that "the long-term performance consequences of voluntary turnover may be less attributable to a skill (human capital) deficit than to the accumulated social capital lost through voluntary turnover."[6] A subsequent test of this supposition with a sample of workers across multiple restaurants provided some empirical support.[7] Variation in restaurant productivity exceeded that which could be explained through basic turnover of human capital alone. The unexplained productivity variance was attributed to disruptions in social capital, indicating that organizations incur costs associated with lost relationships when turnover occurs among individuals that are important to the social network.

8.5.1   Critical Thinking Questions

1. Though organizational social capital enhances the value of an assembled workforce, its contribution to value is difficult to quantify in economic terms. However, employee surveys can provide qualitative insights regarding the extent of organizational social capital present within an organization. What kind of employee survey information might be most relevant for this purpose? Discuss some qualitative indicators of organizational social capital that could be useful for internal decision-making and identify the most informative indicators to report for external stakeholders. Visit the LinkedIn group *The New ROI: Return on Individuals*, hosted by business valuation expert Dave Bookbinder, to glean further insights on this topic from a wide range of disciplines and perspectives.

2. As discussed in this chapter, organizational social capital has many positive benefits, but also some potential negative implications. Reflect on your own experience in the workplace to elaborate on the detrimental possibilities associated with organizational social capital. What are the risks or potential downsides for the organization? Should the valuation of the assembled workforce incorporate

this information in a fashion similar to the positive effects of organizational social capital?

3. The relationships an organization has with its customers or clients are widely recognized as an intangible business asset. It is also generally deemed identifiable, which means there are accepted ways to attribute an economic value to this asset. Why are these external relationships more easily identified and economically quantified than the internal relationships of a business? Reflect on the contractual and transactional nature of the relationship between an organization and its customers or clients. Consider how this differs from the social capital embedded in the quality of the relationships among employees. Finally, discuss why quantitative valuation methods are better suited for evaluating contractual and transactional aspects of relationships than social aspects of relationships.

NOTES

1. Leana, C. R., & Rousseau, D. M. (2000). *Relational wealth: The advantages of stability in a changing economy*. Oxford University Press, USA.
2. Leana, C. R., & Van Buren, H. J. (1999). Organizational social capital and employment practices. *Academy of management review, 24*(3), 538–555.
3. Ibid.
4. Bandiera, O., Barankay, I., & Rasul, I. (2008). Social capital in the workplace: Evidence on its formation and consequences. *Labour Economics, 15*(4), 724–748.
5. Rousseau, D. (1995). *Psychological contracts in organizations: Understanding written and unwritten agreements*. Thousand Oaks, CA: Sage Publications.
6. Dess, G. G., & Shaw, J. D. (2001). Voluntary turnover, social capital, and organizational performance. *Academy of management review, 26*(3), 446–456.
7. Shaw, J. D., Duffy, M. K., Johnson, J. L., & Lockhart, D. E. (2005). Turnover, social capital losses, and performance. *Academy of Management Journal, 48*(4), 594–606.

CHAPTER 9

Other Quantitative Views of Human Capital

Abstract This chapter provides an overview of other quantitative tools for understanding an organization's human capital. The previous chapters examined the overall value of the assembled workforce in place, which is the primary focus of this book. However, economic logic and quantitative measurement are also relevant to examining incremental changes in value associated with human capital practices and for informing human capital strategy decisions. In this chapter, we consider utility analysis, human capital metrics and workforce analytics as ways to evaluate specific aspects of the workforce and human resource practices that ultimately have a bearing on the value of the firm's human capital.

Keywords Utility analysis · Human capital metrics · Workforce analytics Revenue per employee

9.1 INTRODUCTION

There are three prevalent ways to apply a quantitative lens to human resource management: utility analysis, human resource metrics, and statistical workforce analytics. The goal of these approaches is to determine and improve the effectiveness, efficiency, and return associated with human resource initiatives and functions such as training, hiring, turnover, compensation systems, and more. Human resource management related outcomes are most often measured in terms of behavioral

© The Author(s) 2017
K.K. Merriman, *Valuation of Human Capital*,
DOI 10.1007/978-3-319-58934-3_9

outcomes such as employee productivity, rather than in direct financial terms, and when financial measurements are used they are generally cost-based. Certain applications of utility analysis are an exception to this point in that they do consider the financial return on human resource initiatives in terms of the cost–benefit relationship. This chapter provides an overview of each of the three quantitative lenses, utility analysis, human resource metrics, and statistical workforce analysis, in order.

9.2   UTILITY ANALYSIS OVERVIEW

In order to ascribe a monetary value to behavioral outcomes resulting from human resource management initiatives, utility analysis attempts to identify the costs and benefits associated with the specific HR practice. Utility analysis in human resource management originated as an extension of cost accounting principles to the evaluation of employee selection practices in hiring.[1] Many scholars and practitioners have contributed to the extension of utility analysis in human resource management over the years. Wayne Cascio and John Boudreau have been especially impactful in this area and have authored a thorough guide to its application.[2]

In its most straightforward use, utility analysis can determine whether an investment in a particular HR practice results in greater benefits than it costs—i.e., the net financial benefits. However, utility analysis is most useful in making relative comparisons when organizations have a strategic choice between HR practices. The choice may simply be between a new HR approach and the status quo, or can entail consideration of multiple new approaches. Either way, economic rationality dictates the preferred choice is the alternative that provides the highest utility.

Utility analysis is potentially applied to all sorts of HR decisions involving systematic practices to improve employee performance, including hiring methods, training, and even decisions such as whether to permit employees to telecommute or require them to work on site. The primary limitation in applying utility analysis is that the performance outcome resulting from the HR practice of interest must be measurable in incremental units that are convertible to monetary value. For instance, in conducting a utility analysis of a training program, it would first be necessary to determine the incremental change in performance attributable to the training. This part alone may be captured in a relatively straightforward way by comparing pre-training to post-training performance levels. The trickier part is determining the monetary value of this change in performance for the organization.

9.2.1   Utility Analysis Example

Sometimes employee performance is naturally measured in monetizable units, such as widgets produced or widgets sold. Often, however, employee performance is multi-dimensional and less directly connected to the end product. For instance, the job of university professor entails various performance outcomes related to teaching, administrative duties, and scholarly research. High performance might be distinguished from average and poor performance by teaching evaluation scores, administrative committees served, and the number of publications. To convert professor performance to a monetary value for the university, one might estimate how many additional tuition-paying students enroll when professor performance ratings increase or, more precisely, the correlation between student enrollment and professor performance ratings. As you can imagine, student enrollment is influenced by so many factors beyond the professor that isolating the impact of professor performance would be messy at best.

In cases like the above, the compensation associated with the job may be a reasonable proxy for the monetary value of employee performance to the firm. Similar to the cost approach method to valuing human capital that was presented in an earlier chapter, employee pay is generally acknowledged as an indicator of employee value to the firm. For purpose of utility analysis, the average or median compensation for the job can be used. Other creative approaches to estimating the economic value of job performance to the firm are outlined in the Cascio and Boudreau resource referenced earlier in this chapter.

To recap the steps described so far, prior to conducting a utility analysis on any given human resource practice, the analysis will require preliminary attention to:

- A method to measure the degree of impact the human resource practice has on employee performance
- A method to measure the monetary value of employee performance to the firm in incremental units.

Once these minimum data inputs are determined, there are various utility formulas that might be used to conduct an analysis. In addition to impact on performance, the basic utility formula also considers

- The number of employees involved
- The average number of years over which the company will receive the beneficial impact on performance—often based on average employee tenure
- The cost of administering the human resource practice that is driving the beneficial impact on performance.

9.2.2   Finer-Grained Utility Models

Finer-grained utility models have additionally incorporated the time value of money and variable costs associated with performance gains—which speaks to economies or diseconomies of scale, and income tax implications.[3] Models have also considered fluctuations in costs and benefits during the time period in question and different ways of isolating the value of the "status quo" comparison.[4] Similar to the discounted cash flow approach discussed in Chap. 5, a utility analysis can potentially incorporate annual projections of benefits and costs over the estimated relevant time period, and then discount these cash flows to present value. For further insight, a step-by-step example of utility analysis that incorporates many of these refinements can be seen in a research paper by Michael Sturman and colleagues in which they evaluate the comparative utility of three pay strategies.[5]

In practice, this level of detail is ideal but often unattainable due to limited information and the time and cost involved to accurately make such projections. However, often decisions on the use of human resource management practices are aided by simply knowing if the cost is justified, not necessarily the precise return on investment. Utility analysis is well suited for these types of broad brush insights and decisions.

Following is an example of one way to calculate the expected change in utility for a training course (Table 9.1). The change in utility is sufficiently large, such that it would seem benefits would exceed the cost even if granular refinements to the analysis decreased the value of the benefits. In terms of human capital value, the change in utility in this example represents an increase to the economic value of human capital for the organization resulting from enhanced software skills. A cost

Table 9.1   Utility analysis example

Scenario: XYZ Company conducted a software training workshop for a relatively small subset of its data entry employees in order to estimate how training impacts performance before deciding whether to train additional employees.

Formula: Change in Utility = step 1 × step 2 × step 3a × step 3b × step 4 − step 5

1. Number of employees trained   100 employees
2. Average time over which the benefit will continuously occur based on   5 years
   employee turnover estimates
3. Estimate of training impact on performance. Normally a prediction
   of the impact of an HR practice on performance requires an estimate
   of some interim outcome. For example, in this case, training increases
   employee proficiency in use of software, which in turn increases
   performance.
   a. Average "Z-score" of *increased* proficiency after training   1.3
   A Z-score is the individual score, on measurement of increased
   proficiency in this case, minus the mean score for the group,
   divided by the standard deviation. It indicates how many standard
   deviations the score is from the mean, with 0 indicating the popu-
   lation mean.
   b. Correlation between the predictor (software proficiency) and   0.40
   performance (employee performance in data entry)
   Retrospectively, the correlation can be determined through basic
   statistical calculation of the relationship between the predictor
   and the outcome. It is a test of how strongly the two variables are
   related, with 1 indicating a perfect correlation.
4. Value of 1 standard deviation in performance (the value ascribed to a $6000
   1 unit change in the increase in quantity and quality of data entry)
5. Cost of human resource practice (training workshop) $200,000
Change in utility   **$1360,000**
A positive number suggests the training is a worthwhile investment in
that the predicted benefit exceeds the cost. Note, however, that this
predicted amount is derived over 5 years and not discounted to present
value, while the training expense is incurred in year 0 of the analysis.

approach to human capital value would not necessarily reflect this added value unless compensation increased as well, or unless it was reflected as a cure to functional depreciation of the firm's human capital.

9.3   HUMAN CAPITAL METRICS

Human capital metrics represent another way to quantify the relationship between human resource practices and corresponding aspects of human capital. There are an endless potential number of metrics that could be derived, but their purpose could be broadly summed as providing a means for external benchmarking to other organizations or the industry overall, and for internal comparisons and tracking over time. Whereas utility analysis emphasizes the costs and benefits of human resource initiatives in dollar terms, human capital metrics emphasize efficiency and return on investment expressed as relative ratios that translate easily for comparison purposes.

As said, there are a multitude of metrics associated with the various aspects of human resource management. The Human Capital Management Handbook touts over 620 human capital measures for companies to consider. These metrics include the categories of recruiting and hiring, training, leadership and development, engagement, productivity and performance, compensation and benefits, headcount, mobility and career development, turnover and retention, and more.[6]

9.3.1   Metrics for Productivity and Investment in Human Capital

Productivity itself is interpreted in a variety of ways. Productivity is defined as the level of *output* achieved for a given level of *input*.[7] A recent World at Work interview with a leading consultant in this area provided an overview on productivity measures.[8] Outputs of particular interest include revenue and products sold. Common inputs include number of hours worked and number of employees in a given role. For instance, a greater number of products sold per employee in period 2 relative to period 1 indicate an increase in productivity. Productivity may also be measured as efficiency (e.g., units produced per worker), quality (e.g., the number of errors per widget), customer service (e.g., customer retention per account representative), and more. Productivity measures are also tailored to the industry and job (e.g., number of patients seen per physician). Productivity measures provide a way to track progress over time, progress in relation to a set target, and standing in relation to competitors and peer organizations.

The Society for Human Resource Management references some standard metrics pertaining to compensation and training, both of which speak to a company's ongoing investment in human capital.[9] For instance, the cost efficiency of compensation is reflected in the ratio of compensation costs to revenue or to total operating costs. The relative degree of investments in employee training is expressed as total training costs as a ratio of total employees or total operating expenses. Similarly, one way to view the return on investment (ROI) in human capital is the ratio of net revenue to total compensation costs.

9.3.2   Revenue Per Employee

For external comparison of the impact and efficiency of human capital in relation to the organization's financial performance, revenue per employee is arguably one of the most useful ratios.[10] Revenue per employee is calculated by dividing total revenue by the number of employees during the revenue period. This figure is normally based on an annual period and can be calculated in three basic steps as follows.

1. First, determine the average total number of full-time equivalent employees (FTE) for the year. Firms that hire part-time workers will need to convert these hours to full-time equivalent by adding the total part-time hours engaged during the year and dividing by 2080 h (the equivalent of a 40-h work week for 52 weeks). For firms in which the number of full-time employees fluctuated throughout the year, an average estimate can be derived by taking the total number of employees in place at each quarter throughout the year, summing these numbers and dividing by four.
2. Next, determine which measures of revenue are most insightful for your particular business and industry. External benchmarks are readily available for total revenue per employee and net income per employee. For example, CSIMarket.com is a free online resource for these data by sector, industry, and public company.
3. Divide total revenue or net income by the average number of FTE employees for comparison to external benchmarks. For internal purposes, revenue per employee provides an average indication of value potentially lost if an employee leaves the organization.

Carrying the training example from utility analysis to our discussion of human capital metrics, we would expect the revenue-per-employee metric to improve after training. That is, holding all else constant, an increase in revenue per employee indicates that the firm's human capital has become more productive or efficient in generating revenue. A declining revenue-per-employee ratio, again holding all other internal and external market factors constant, may indicate a need for employee training or a decrease in employee motivation and engagement. However, care must be taken to also consider fluctuations in market conditions as a source of changing revenues. One way to adjust for broad market influences is to deduct the industry average revenue per employee from the firm's metric to focus on the change beyond variations in the market.

It is also informative to compare the firm's revenue-per-employee metric to external benchmarks. If a given company generates more revenue per employee than its competitors, they are doing a better job in leveraging their human capital assets. However, care must be given when making external comparisons beyond highly similar firms since the metric varies widely based on the nature of the work. Labor-intensive industries with many lower skilled workers such as the restaurant industry averaged $53,544 in revenue per employee for 2016, whereas the internet services and social media industry averaged $1590,710 in revenue per employee for the same time period, based on CSIMarket.com tracking of companies publicly traded in the United States.

Replacing revenue per employee with net income ("profit") per employee removes the potentially wide variations across firms in the cost required to support employees' work and therefore allows for a broader comparison of companies. Still, higher profit per employee is only one way to improve company's financial performance.[11] Financial performance also relies on the number of employees generating that profit. A million dollars in profit per employee in a firm with 10 employees equates to $10 million in profit. A $30,000 profit per employee in a firm with 1000 employees equates to $30 million in profit. As with any human capital metric, revenue and profit per employee is still only one piece of overall human capital value.

9.4   Workforce Analytics

Workforce analytics is the use of empirical data—information derived through observation and experimentation—by organizational decision-makers to improve the management of an organization's human resources. The term more broadly involves identifying key issues for empirical analysis, research design, data collection, statistical analysis, and articulating findings in a practical way.[12]

As depicted in Fig. 9.1, empirical data is derived from sources such as employee surveys, experiments, employee records, and more. Research design follows two broad approaches. An inductive, bottom-up approach searches for patterns in data and is well suited to exploring "big" data,

Workforce analytics is the use of empirical data by organizational decision makers to improve the management of an organization's human resources.

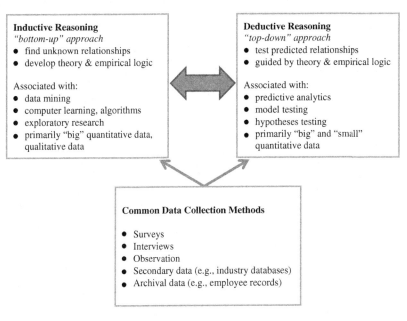

Inductive Reasoning
"bottom-up" approach
- find unknown relationships
- develop theory & empirical logic

Associated with:
- data mining
- computer learning, algorithms
- exploratory research
- primarily "big" quantitative data, qualitative data

Deductive Reasoning
"top-down" approach
- test predicted relationships
- guided by theory & empirical logic

Associated with:
- predictive analytics
- model testing
- hypotheses testing
- primarily "big" and "small" quantitative data

Common Data Collection Methods

- Surveys
- Interviews
- Observation
- Secondary data (e.g., industry databases)
- Archival data (e.g., employee records)

Fig. 9.1 Workforce analytics overview

in other words, extremely large datasets, to discover previously unknown relationships among the data. A deductive, top-down approach tests predicted relationships to confirm and extend existing knowledge. An important advantage to the latter approach is the close consideration of the causal logic underlying the relationship patterns. Consider the following:

> Say that in your role as a research scientist you analyzed the sleep habits of thousands of individuals and discovered a conclusive finding. When individuals slept with their shoes on, they were significantly more likely to wake in the morning with a headache. What practical advice could you take from this finding to help the public?

If you thought of advising the public that sleeping with shoes on leads to headaches, you have fallen for the trap of mistaking correlation for causality. Reflecting more deeply on the causal logic, it should occur to you that there is an underlying variable that could explain both the shoes and the headache—collapsing into bed after a night of heavy drinking.

To empirically confirm theorized causality requires a research design in which the effect occurs after the causal factor, and other plausible explanations for the cause–effect relationship are eliminated. This type of research control is attained through research experiments (useful resources on experimental research fundamentals for beginners include Chap. 3 of Cascio and Boudreau's previously referenced book[13] and a Harvard Business Review article on business experiments[14]). For instance, the training example discussed at the start of this chapter for utility analysis was inherently set up as an experiment by testing employee proficiency (the effect) before and after the training (the cause). Further, the subset of similar employees not receiving training serves as a "control" group to help eliminate the possibility that other unknown organizational factors are driving the result. In turn, these findings show if and how behavior changed, and provide the unit of behavioral change needed to conduct utility analysis.

Laszlo Bock, the former head of "people operations" at Google during their reign as pioneers in systematically conducting and applying empirical research to human resource management, noted that simple analytics can provide great insights.[15] Indeed, controlled tests of narrowed predictions are the backbone of causal insights. Basic approaches to data analysis include tests of correlation involving two variables (bivariate correlation), multivariate regression analysis, and comparison of means to determine if groups significantly vary from one another on some relevant outcome—particularly useful for experimental research designs.

These basic analyses can be conducted within Excel, or through user-friendly statistical software packages such as SPSS by IBM. However, there is a science and art to research design, data collection, and interpreting and presenting findings that is not to be taken for granted. Organizations and individuals that are serious in applying workforce analytics must develop or hire the expertise needed in these areas.

9.4.1   Critical Thinking Questions

1. Is there a potential downside to a relatively high revenue-to-employee ratio? In other words, can an organization be too efficient in doing more with less when it comes to human resources?

Discuss the potential advantage in having slack or spare resources in the area of human productivity when it comes to adapting to unforeseen productivity demands and future growth.
2. This chapter gave an example of a training experiment to test the effect of training on employee proficiency. Think about other human resource management practices that are well suited for experimental, cause–effect testing. Describe how you might design an experiment around a specific human resource practice.
3. Imagine you are an investor considering buying a large number of shares in a particular company. The firm has supplemented their financial reporting with the following metrics: investment in training per employee and revenue per employee. Your comparison of this information to industry benchmarks suggests both metrics are very low. How would this influence your evaluation of the organization and decision to invest? Discuss the relationship between investment in training and employee productivity.

NOTES

1. Brogden, H. E., & Taylor, E. K. (1950). The dollar criterion—applying the cost accounting concept to criterion construction. *Personnel Psychology*, *3*(2), 133–154. Also see Brogden, H. E. (1946). On the interpretation of the correlation coefficient as a measure of predictive efficiency. *Journal of educational psychology*, *37*(2), 65; Brogden, H. E. (1949). When testing pays off. *Personnel Psychology*, *2*(2), 171–183.
2. Cascio, W. F., & Boudreau, J. W. (2011). *Investing in People: Financial Impact of Human Resource Initiatives* (2nd ed). Upper Saddle River, NJ: Pearson Education.
3. Boudreau, J. W. (1983). Economic considerations in estimating the utility of human resource productivity improvement programs. *Personnel Psychology*, *36*(3), 551–576.
4. Sturman, M. C. (2000). Implications of utility analysis adjustments for estimates of human resource intervention value. *Journal of Management*, *26*(2), 281–299.
5. Sturman, M. C., Trevor, C. O., Boudreau, J. W., & Gerhart, B. (2003). Is it worth it to win the talent war? Evaluating the utility of performance-based pay. *Personnel Psychology*, *56*(4), 997–1035.
6. Human Capital Management Institute (2012). *Human Capital Management Handbook* (2nd ed). Marina Del Rey, CA: HCMI.
7. O'Leonard, K. (2017, January 10). Defining and measuring workforce effectiveness and productivity. In *World at Work Workspan Weekly*,

World at Work TV. Retrieved from: https://www.worldatwork.org/ adimLink?id=81085&utm_source=Direct&utm_medium=eNewsletter& utm_term=ww_editorial2_ls_subscribe_wkspan_wkly_b1&utm_ content=Video&utm_campaign=ED_ANWLWKS0217.

8. Ibid.
9. Weatherly, L. A. (2003, September). The value of people: The challenges and opportunities of human capital measurement and reporting. *Society for Human Resource Management Research Quarterly.*
10. Bryan, L. L. (2007, February). The new metrics of corporate performance: Profit per employee. *McKinsey Quarterly.* Retrieved from http://www.mckinsey.com/business-functions/strategy-and-corporate-finance/our-insights/the-new-metrics-of-corporate-performance-profit-per-employee.
11. Ibid.
12. Cascio, W. F., & Boudreau, J. W. Ibid.
13. Ibid.
14. Davenport, T. H. (2009). How to design smart business experiments. *Harvard Business Review, 87*(2), 68–76.
15. Laszlo, B. (2015). Work rules: Insights from inside Google that will transform how you live and lead. New York, NY: Hachette Book Group.

INDEX

© The Editor(s) (if applicable) and The Author(s) 2017
K.K. Merriman, *Valuation of Human Capital*,
DOI 10.1007/978-3-319-58934-3

CPSIA information can be obtained
at www.ICGtesting.com
Printed in the USA
LVOW13*1952271017

554038LV00014B/325/P